SOCK DOLL WORKSHOP

SOCK DOLL WORKSHOP

30 Delightful Dolls
To Create and Cherish

CINDY CRANDALL-FRAZIER

Lark Books

Acknowledgments

I would like to thank everyone at Altamont Press for their enthusiasm, with special thanks to my editor, Bobbe Needham, for her friendship and sense of humor as well as her editing skill. I am happy to, with this book and within its pages, thank my parents for raising my brothers and me in an atmosphere where the work of hands was respected.

Thanks to my husband, Richard, for his support throughout the process and to my daughter, Naomi, who believed this book would find a publisher.

Published in 1995 by Lark Books
50 College Street
Asheville, North Carolina, U.S.A. 28801

Editor: Bobbe Needham

Art Director: Chris Colando

Production: Chris Colando

Photograpy: Evan Bracken

ISBN 0-937274-94-1

Library of Congress Cataloging-in-Publication Data available

Printed in Hong Kong.

Contents

Introduction

When I was a child, my grandmother made some of those hunting-sock monkeys. They fascinated me, yet dolls were my love, and I couldn't understand why I never saw one as cleverly wrought as those monkeys. Years later in a small gift shop in Pennsylvania, I found among a cluster of handmade Amish dolls one made from a white sock and dressed in the somber wovens of her sect. To my eyes, her round knittedness gave her a soft appeal that the others lacked.

At some point I began to visualize odd pieces of miniature clothing whenever I looked at socks. A terry-lined sport sock, for instance, looked to me like a baby's sleep suit. I noticed that the tops of socks resembled the bottoms of small sweaters, and I imagined the ribbing of a bright blue sock becoming a little ski hat.

I have always been intrigued by the process by which a designer moves from vision to creation. The vision of sock figures in sock clothing came to me one day as I stood before a colorful array of socks in a department store. In my mind's eye, the socks came apart and rejoined in new ways or combined with other socks. As I watched, colors, shapes, and patterns seemed to shift, suggesting more and more variations. I bought several pairs of socks and went home to get my hands involved in this vision—to begin transforming imagination into reality.

I have designed and made other kinds of dolls, but I have never experienced the pure fun that creating these soft, squishy sock dolls has afforded me. I hope everyone who encounters this book will taste the enjoyment I have had and, better yet, go on to entertain their own visions and create something entirely new, all their own.

About the Dolls

Merry Anne, So Big the Bear, Ti Nee—I believe that the appealing simplicity of the dolls in this book will endear them not only to children but to collectors and crafters as well. For as easy as the dolls are to make, they represent a remarkable range, from tiny Cradle Baby and the huggable Pocket Pals to elegant Margot the Ballerina and the playful cardinal, dinosaur, and lion Costume Kids.

Using socks as the key source of fabric and fashioning the clothing as an integral part of each doll both simplifies construction and allows plenty of freedom to experiment with the possibilities of socks. Cutting and sewing is faster, and little fabric is wasted.

With minor adjustments, you can recreate the dolls in any size for which you can find appropriate socks. The most common sock size, nine to eleven, which generally offers the greatest variety, makes dolls that average a cuddly fifteen inches (38.5 cm) tall. I've chosen to put hats on many of the dolls, eliminating the need for hair, but you may prefer them with curls, pigtails, or crew cuts. You may want to make up whole families of dolls quickly and easily to fill children's needs for role play— small figures for block play, babies for loving, family units for exploring relationships.

Once you see how easy and fun making these dolls is, you may find yourself lingering in sock departments checking for intriguing colors, patterns, and stitches. Simply varying trims produces a new creation every time. If you are a collector or crafter of folk art, you may find yourself especially drawn to Santa, Fergus the Fisherman, Merry Anne (the rag doll), and Socko the Clown. Any one of these figures can become a hobby in itself, different sock patterns and faces bringing new characters to life with each metamorphosis.

Perhaps you will choose to create some of the dolls as gifts, designed for a particular friend or child— although giving them away may prove more difficult than you imagine. My intention with this book is simply to offer a framework, a pattern, for you to breathe life into.

Starting Out

Gathering Your Materials

One of the great advantages of creating sock dolls is that this craft doesn't take up a lot of space or use exotic, hard-to-find materials. The basic tool chest includes thread in colors to match the socks, two or three fine 1½" (4 cm) needles, scissors, a handful of straight pins, and a ruler. For doll faces, you'll need embroidery floss, a small set of acrylic paints and paint brushes, or both. To make dolls with hair, add a wide-toothed comb, yarn, a spool of carpet thread, and a hair loom (more on this later). For the dinosaur Costume Kid and dolls with boy or baby haircuts, a hot-glue gun comes in handy, but even in these cases you may find sewing just as easy. I use a basket, lunch box, or small plastic tote to keep everything together and make straightening up easier. You'll also need stuffing and, of course, a variety of colorful socks.

Most projects in the book call for hand sewing. You can stitch lengthwise seams either by hand or machine, but where machine stitching does a better job, I've noted this on the projects.

SOCK TIP:

Even though most socks are preshrunk and colorfast, it's a good idea to prewash socks with an unfamiliar manufacturer's label. All the dolls are hand washable, if treated with care, and you can pop the simpler ones inside a large white sock, pillowcase, or lingerie bag and machine wash and dry them as you would any delicate washable.

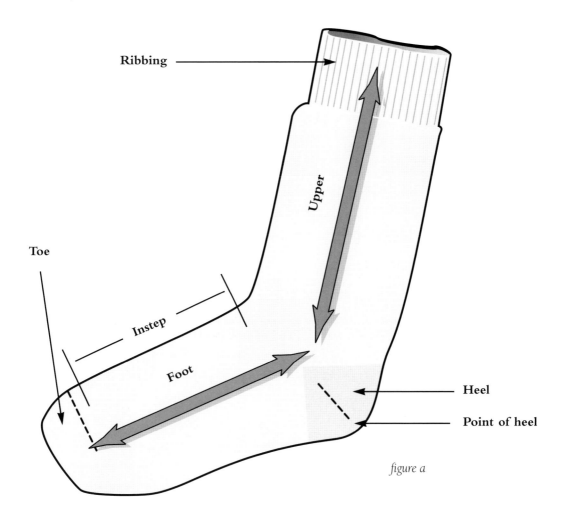

Ribbing

Upper

Toe

Instep

Foot

Heel

Point of heel

figure a

Shopping for Socks

There are a few things to keep in mind when you shop for socks. I find that natural fibers make a doll pleasing to the touch, and luckily most socks are made of cotton. On some projects, cotton socks without any synthetic elasticity work best because they allow the dolls' skirts to drape—in each case, I've noted this in the project instructions. For Fergus, So Big, and Terry, synthetic fibers provide an appealing alternative. The socks for Fergus's trousers are a synthetic blend that looks like wool, but they cost less than wool socks. So Big the Bear is made from a pair of acrylic fiber socks that give him some fuzziness and stretch. Synthetic and cotton fibers combine to make Terry's soft, stretchy sleeper.

Before you buy, you can check the sock weave for tightness by stretching the socks across the knitting. If large gaps appear between the threads, stuffing will show through. For anklets and crew socks, you can also stretch across the ribbing to get

an idea of what the finished doll will look like (see fig. a for sock parts). Some ribbing becomes almost flat when stretched or stuffed, while some stays tight and well defined—which you choose depends on what kind of look you're after.

Depending on where you live, you'll probably find that some kinds and colors of socks vary with the seasons. At back-to-school time, more knee socks usually show up on store counters. As Christmas approaches, you'll find a wider selection of socks that will make great sweaters for Santa, and spring brings a bouquet of pastels.

I avoid socks with advertising printed on the feet or knitted into the design. (For Pearl and Fergus, this is a consideration for their bodies only; you discard the foot bottoms of the socks used for their sweaters.)

The availability of socks for making dolls with a range of skin tones may vary by season and locale. For the most part I've used white socks for the

heads, because they provide the widest range of fabric quality and are easier to find packaged at bargain prices. More socks are being left in natural cotton colors (Patty's head is made from a natural cotton sock), which offer a variety of shades. Heads for dolls with lighter skin tones can also be made with pale peach, pale pink, or cream-colored socks, and oriental dolls can be made from socks in shades of tan and golden brown. African American characters are best made from light tan to chocolate brown shades, because it's harder to apply a realistic-looking face on very dark fabric. If you plan to make a number of dolls in ethnic shades, it's a good idea to shop around and stock up in advance on socks for their heads and bodies.

Stuffing Heads and Bodies

You can create great variety in your dolls depending on the amount of stuffing you use in their heads, bodies, and limbs, and on how firmly you stuff them. Use any good polyester stuffing for the dolls in this book.

Heads

Because a sock of any shape will serve for a head (where heads from separate socks are called for) as long as the knit is smooth on the foot, I haven't drawn diagrams of those socks. Cutting lines for heads are not shown on any of the projects because where to cut varies according to the size of the sock, how stretchy it is, and how firmly you stuff it. Leaving the sock whole while you stuff the head gives you more leverage for packing and prevents frayed edges. To make stuffing easier, fold the upper down once or twice.

To stuff a head, start with an amount of stuffing that seems larger than the finished head should be.

 **SOCK TIP:**

I have always made the heads of my dolls before the bodies, so I've written the instructions for each project in that order. If you have trouble getting correct head/body proportion, try shaping the body first and then stuffing the head to match.

Push it firmly into the toe of the intended sock, forming the face on the side without the toe seam. Continue pressing in smaller amounts of stuffing, turning the sock and rearranging stuffing to achieve a smooth look.

Heads for child and adult dolls differ. For a child doll, arrange one of the last puffs of stuffing toward the lower face to create a cheeky look and at the same time provide a nape. After you have shaped the head, stuff the neck area loosely to give it body and keep the head from flopping. Run a gathering stitch around the neck, draw it up, and knot off. Trim away the excess sock, leaving about half an inch (1 cm) below the gathering.

Adult doll heads should be thinner and more egg shaped than those for child dolls. When you have formed the desired shape, push in a bit of stuffing to stiffen the neck. Sew a gathering stitch around the neck, running the stitching high across the back of the head and low across the front. Knot off, then trim away the excess sock as for the child doll, leaving about half an inch (1.5 cm) below the gathering. Make the chin more prominent by levering stuffing into it with the point of a needle inserted in the side of the face.

SOCK TIP:

Often you can make two heads from a straight-knit sports sock—after you've made one head, trim the cut edge of the sock piece remaining, gather it closed, and stuff it so that the heel becomes the doll's cheeks. These second heads with seams at the crown will need to be covered by hats or hair. (You can make more than two heads from a straight-knit knee sock.)

SOCK TIP:

Once a hand is stuffed, running a gathering thread around the top helps keep the stuffing in and makes it easier to sew the hand to the arm.

Hands

Hands are easy to measure and can be cut from any convenient fabric left from the sock used for the head, so I have not drawn cutting lines for them on the project diagrams. With larger socks, enough fabric for both hands sometimes remains below the heel after you have stuffed the toe for the head. On some projects you can cut one hand from the straight knitting on the heel and another from the instep fabric directly opposite the heel. Socks with a knit or printed pattern starting high on the upper (this is often true of crew socks) sometimes have enough fabric for hands between the heel area and the pattern. You can also cut hands from the ribbing of leftover uppers when the ribbing is very fine.

If you decide to make any of the dolls in the book in different sizes, here's a tip for hand dimensions: use $1\frac{1}{2}$ x 2" (4 x 5 cm) rectangles when you make the bodies from adult-sized socks or from larger children's sizes; use $1\frac{1}{4}$ x $1\frac{3}{4}$" (3.5 x 4.5 cm) rectangles when you make bodies from small children's or babies' socks. (It's easier to alter hand size by using different amounts of stuffing than by cutting hands of different dimensions for every size change.)

Bodies

As with any soft-sculpture figures, you can vary the body type of these sock dolls by how much stuffing you use and how firmly you stuff the doll. To create a longer, more slender body, press small amounts of stuffing in firmly. For a more rounded figure, loosely pack in larger amounts of stuffing. With extra bits of stuffing, you can create knees, elbows, and chins. Don't be shy about playing around with stuffing techniques.

For a doll without separated legs, you'll stuff the body in much the same way you stuff a head. Start with an amount of stuffing that will round out the toe of the sock, then continue packing in smaller

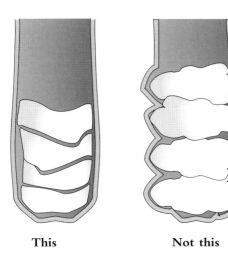

This   **Not this**

figure b

SOCK TIP:

You may want to use a dowel to stuff long legs. The sides of the dowel should be smooth to prevent snags, but leave the end rough so that it will grip the stuffing.

bits. End with enough stuffing to pad the shoulders when the head is seated.

For dolls with legs, the trick is to stuff evenly, being careful not to twist the leg or wad the stuffing into a ball (fig. b). I often leave a gap without stuffing at the top of each leg to allow movement in the legs after I've stuffed the rest of the body. (I've included specific instructions with the projects for stuffing the legs of dolls with feet that bend forward.)

When a doll's rear is formed by the heel of the sock, use a large piece of stuffing to make it smooth and round before continuing to work up the torso.

To prepare to seat a head, I find it works best to reach into the stuffed torso with the first two fin-

gers of each hand and pull the top stuffing from the center to both shoulders. This creates a cavity for the head and builds up the shoulder area at the same time.

I prefer lightly stuffed arms for the babies, medium firmness for the children, and considerable firmness for the adults and So Big the Bear. As with the legs, it's important not to twist the arms while stuffing.

Designing Faces

For your first dolls, I think you'll find simple shapes most effective for facial features: circles, half circles, triangles, dots, and lines. For instance, I used rectangles to make Ti Nee's oriental eyes, half circles for Emily's and the Pocket Pals' eyes, and a circle with lines on each side for many of the mouths. I encourage you to try variations as you gain confidence.

Mark the positions of facial features lightly with a pencil, placing babies' and children's eyes about midway down the face, adults' eyes higher.

Unlike embroidery floss, acrylic and fabric-marker paint are just about impossible to remove once you have applied them. The instructions for each project call for designing the faces last because that is when you'll have the best sense of your character, but if you feel a little unsure of yourself or don't want to take any chances, consider painting faces on the heads before seating them on the bodies—you can always make another head if you need to.

Paint

If you intend to paint a number of faces, you'll find it worthwhile to purchase quality brushes and paints. Acrylic paints work best for painting on fabric and will be permanent when dry. In brushes, look for artists' brands with red sable, white nylon,

Before you actually paint a face, practice on scraps of fabric. Then you'll know how wet your brush needs to be for a good line—if it's too wet, the paint will run. I keep a blotter handy when I paint.

Thin the mix with water before you apply it. Upper lips need to be darker than lower lips, as they are more shadowed. For a wet look, you can blend in a small accent of white on lower lips.

For rosy cheeks, brush-on blush works well (I keep a blush for dolls only). If you intend to give the doll to a younger child (who is likely to chew on it), either omit blush or lightly rub some watered-down mouth color on the cheeks with a cotton ball. You can use the same technique for other dolls or use brush-on blush.

Fabric Markers

I find fabric markers faster and easier to use than either paint or embroidery floss, but I prefer paint and floss because they offer a wider range of color.

or sabeline bristles. The handles should be short: six or seven inches (15-18 cm). Bristle size varies slightly from company to company. I use a size three brush for making eyes and mouths and a size zero for details.

To make blue eyes, I use ultramarine blue, thinning the paint with water until I get a color about the shade of a ripe blueberry. After you've painted both eyes blue, mix a small amount of blue with titanium white and with it make a curved line in the lower half of each eye. Then with a tiny brush, make highlights with a dot of plain white in the upper right and lower left of each eye.

For brown eyes I mix ultramarine blue, napthol crimson, and cadmium yellow, then thin the resulting brown. Paint the eyes on, then mix a little brown with white or yellow and make a curved line inside the lower half of each eye. For dark-colored eyes, a separate pupil isn't essential, but you can add one with a touch of black paint. With a smaller brush and white only, highlight the upper right and lower left of each eye.

For the mouth, I create a nice red orange by mixing napthol crimson and a little cadmium yellow.

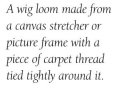

SOCK TIP:

When I paint, I lay the wet brushes I'm not using at the moment on a flat surface to avoid bending the bristles. Cool water works best for rinsing brushes after use, because warm water can cause bristles to come unglued.

Several brands of fabric markers are permanent when dry. As a double check, though, it's a good idea to paint a sample head with the fabric markers you intend to use and put it through a wash-and-dry cycle.

To make blue eyes, draw and fill in the eye shapes with a light-blue marker. Outline the eyes and fill in the upper halves with a dark blue. For brown eyes, make the first layer yellow, then outline the eyes and fill in the upper halves with brown. You can make green eyes with light green as the base color and dark green or black to darken. For all eyes, add black for the pupils and white acrylic paint for the highlights.

You can draw eyelashes and brows with the tip of a fresh marker (worn or drying markers don't work for details), although I find that lightly embroidered lashes and brows add a nice touch.

figure c

A wig loom made from a canvas stretcher or picture frame with a piece of carpet thread tied tightly around it.

A wig loom made from a simple, notched piece of heavy cardboard with the carpet thread tied firmly around it at the notches.

Draw the mouth with yellow or orange and apply pink or red over that base. You can rub a dot of white acrylic paint on the lower lip for gloss.

Embroidery Floss

Cut easy-to-handle lengths of embroidery floss. Thread a needle with three strands of floss for eyes or mouth, one strand for eyelashes and brows. Stitch into the head, bringing the needle out where you plan to start embroidering, leaving a few inches of thread inside the head. To secure the thread, take a tiny stitch at the beginning of each feature. When you finish embroidering a feature, take another tiny stitch, then insert the needle close to the last stitch and bring it out a few inches away. Carefully cut the thread flush with the face.

The only two stitches you need to embroider faces are the satin stitch and the backstitch: the satin stitch works for all features, and a backstitch (or stem stitch) makes a smiling mouth. For example, I used satin stitch for So Big's eyes and nose, Merry Anne's eyes and nose, and the Beach Buddies' eyes and mouths, and backstitched lines for So Big's and Merry Anne's mouths. I added two tiny white stitches in each eye for highlights.

Making Hair

You can weave a simple wig of straight hair on a hair loom, which is easy and inexpensive to make—all you need is carpet thread and either a canvas stretcher or a piece of heavy cardboard. (Available at art supply stores, a canvas stretcher is a simple frame used by artists to stretch canvas for painting.) A loom 10 x 12" (26 x 31 cm) will do for any project in this book. Tie the thread around the stretcher or cardboard. If you use cardboard, notch it on each side about two inches (5 cm) from the top to prevent the thread from slipping and reinforce the notches with strong tape to keep the thread from cutting into the cardboard as you're working (fig. c).

To make a yarn wig on a loom, follow the diagrams here.

I give suggestions for strand length and wig length in the instructions for specific projects.

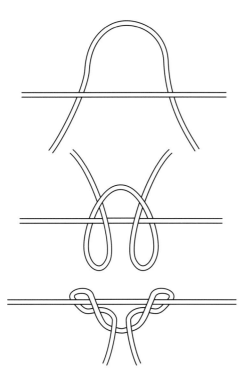

figure d

The horizontal line represents the carpet thread on the hair loom. Begin the wig by cutting a strand of yarn and folding it in half. Hold the fold behind the carpet thread.

Bring the two ends forward under the carpet thread and back over it, through the loop created by the fold of yarn. Tug on the ends of yarn to tighten the knot.

Push each new knotted strand up against the last one. The more tightly packed the knots, the thicker the wig.

Creating Curls

To make curly hair, wrap yarn around a dowel to form coils. (The instructions for Merry Anne call for wrapping yarn around a ruler; you can also use a pencil, magic marker, or wooden spoon handle instead of a dowel.) After wrapping the needed length along the dowel, backstitch through the yarn along one side. Then gently pull the coil of yarn off the dowel, being careful not to twist it. Overcast the coil in place on the doll's head, sewing through the line of backstitching, the yarn, and the head. Repeat for as many coils as you need to cover the head (fig. e).

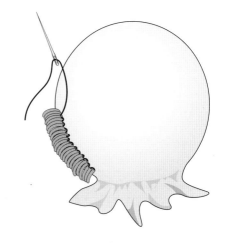

figure e

Stitches

For the projects in the book, the **backstitch** is the best stitch for seams and for sewing coils of yarn together for curly hair. You can also use it to embroider mouths. Embroider simple but effective loop curls on babies by clustering several **daisy stitches**. Use the **ladder stitch** to attach heads to bodies and hands to arms and to stitch feet in a forward position.

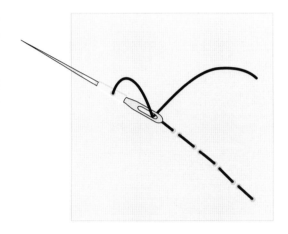

Backstitch

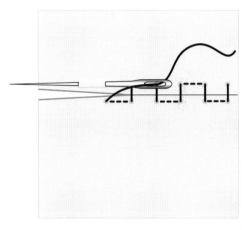

Ladder Stitch

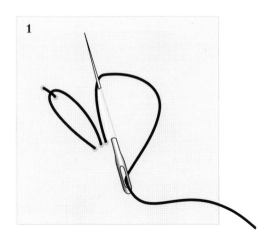

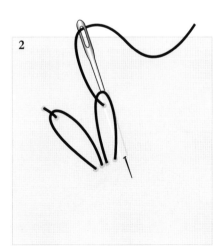

Daisy Stitch

To sew Fergus's boots and Pearl's shoes, use an *overcast stitch*. A slightly modified overcast stitch is used to attach the edge of one piece to the flat of another. For example, to attach a hat to a head, pick up a small stitch of head fabric with the needle each time before taking a stitch in the edge of the hat. The *running* or *gathering stitch* works best for gathering, as on necks and hands. It can also be used as an alternative to the backstitch for sewing simple seams, although the backstitch is the better choice.

Use *satin stitch* to shape eyes, noses, and mouths. To sew through thick pieces, use a *stab stitch*, which is a running stitch made one step at a time. Embroider smiling mouths with a *stem stitch*—be sure the needle exits each stitch on the outside of the curve. *Tacking* is taking a couple of stitches to hold a piece in place.

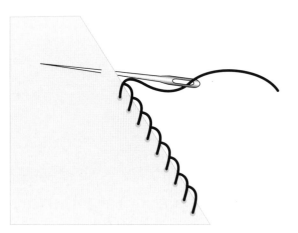

Overcast Stitch

Satin Stitch

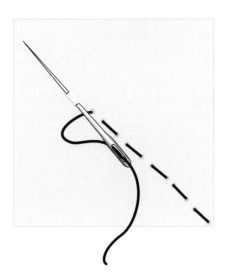

Running Stitch

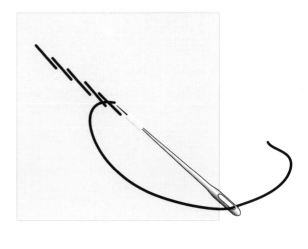

Stem Stitch

SOCK TIP:

At the end of every step, after knotting your thread, insert your needle close to the knot and bring it back out an inch or two away, thus hiding the tail in the stuffing. Cut the thread off close to the fabric.

Some Basic Steps in Construction

You won't need all six of the steps in this section for every doll, and in some projects you'll repeat a step—for example, attaching the hands calls for the same technique as attaching ball feet. Instructions for the more complex dolls have additional diagrams with the projects.

Directions for this project begin on page 56.

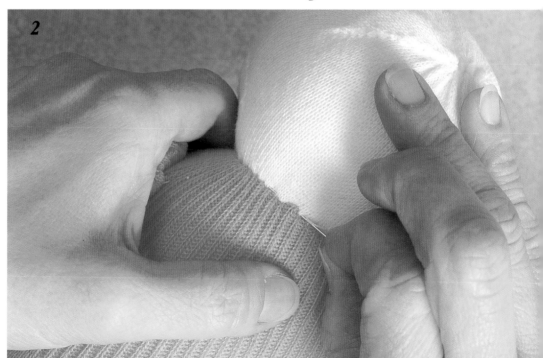

1 Ladder Stitching a Foot

Prepare a needle and thread. Remove the pin that separates the foot from the leg. Bend the foot forward and, holding it in position, insert the needle in the crease so the knot won't show. Bring the needle out at the ankle. Ladder stitch across the outside of the crease. Stop occasionally to tighten the stitches by pulling the thread up. The seam should be smooth and firm but not puckered. Turn the work around and stitch back across for strength. Knot off.

2 Ladder Stitching the Head to the Body

This step comes after you have run a gathering thread around the top of the torso, seated the head, and drawn up the gathering thread while tucking the seam allowance inside. If the leftover gathering thread is long enough, use it to attach the head to the body. If not, thread a needle and insert it under a bit of seam allowance at the back of the head so the knot won't show. Hold the head in place and ladder stitch the seam. Stop occasionally to draw the stitches up firmly. Sewing twice around the neck makes a strong seam. Knot off at the back.

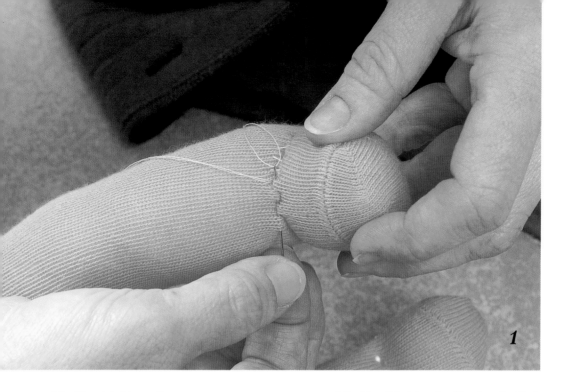

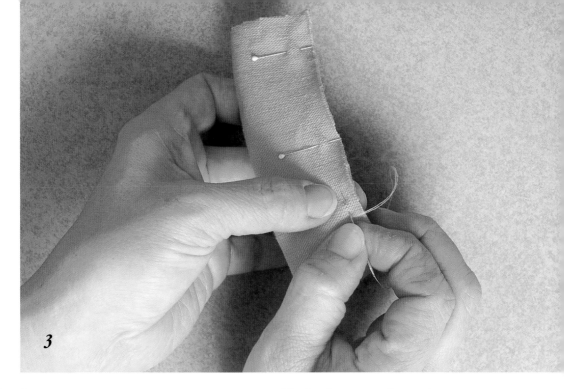

3

3 Backstitching an Arm Seam

Fold the arm so that the right sides are together. A few well-positioned pins will make the job easier. Arm and leg seams can be stitched on a sewing machine, but backstitching will leave more ease for the fabric to stretch when it is stuffed.

4 Ladder Stitching a Hand to an Arm

This step comes after you have turned the arm right side out, run a gathering thread around one end of the arm, inserted the unfinished end of the hand, and drawn up the gathering thread while tucking the seam allowance inside. With the remaining gathering thread, ladder stitch the hand to the arm. If the doll is to be given to a young child, it is especially important to work more than once around the hand and to make a strong knot, so the child can't pull the hand off.

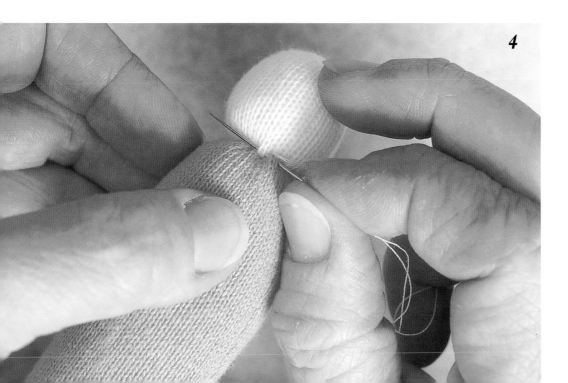

4

5

5 Sewing an Arm to a Body

Place the arm against the body with the arm seam running under the arm and the top opening flattened at the shoulder. Some projects call for gathering the upper arm loosely, and some do not. If a gathering thread has been run, use the remaining thread to sew the arm to the body. If not, after turning in the seam allowance, thread a needle and insert it under the seam allowance, bringing it out at the fold at the right side of the arm. Overcast across the top of the arm, picking up torso fabric and both sides of the arm opening in every stitch. (If the torso has more than one layer of fabric, try to pick up both.) Work back across for a strong seam, and knot off.

SOCK TIP:

Whenever you need to gather a tube of fabric to a close, as with the ends of hands and the tops of hats, overcast across the opening that remains to make sure the seam allowance doesn't get pushed to the outside.

6 Overcasting a Hat to a Head

If the hat tends to slip out of position on the head, pin it in place. Thread a needle and insert it into the seam allowance or cuff of the hat at the back of the head so the knot won't show. Make small overcast stitches, catching both the head and the hat. Work all the way around and knot off.

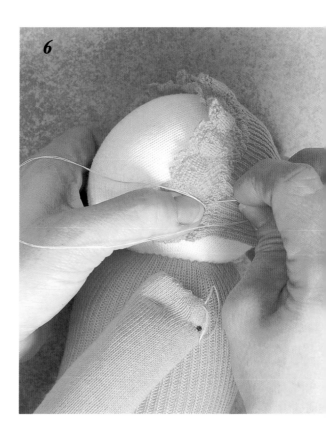

6

A Last Word on Technique

Use the project's written instructions rather than the diagrams as your main source for how to make a doll, because they include more detail than the diagrams can show. For each project the diagrams show the style of sock that inspired the project, but the instructions allow you to experiment with other styles.

Seams

Seam allowances are usually $\frac{1}{4}$" (1 cm) for legs, arms, and gathered edges on bodies. When a narrow seam is called for it should be $\frac{1}{8}$" (0.5 cm). I usually recommend a width of $\frac{1}{8}$" for the seam opposite the fold on the hands. As with any craft, though, no hard-and-fast rules apply. Your fabric will dictate some of your decisions about seam allowances because of its density of stitches, fraying tendencies, and stretchability.

Proportions

At two points during construction, you may need to make adjustments to improve proportion. The first comes before you seat the head, when you need to

SOCK TIP:

Save yourself future frustration and expense by labeling the sock size of left-over pieces with self-stick dots, the sock labels, or masking tape.

check to see that the torso isn't too long. When you gather the top of the body around the head, the torso should be about the same length as the legs. The legs can be longer for effect on some figures, but a long torso with short legs looks awkward.

The second adjustment point concerns the arms: hold them in position against the body before sewing them on. If the tips of the hands fall below midthigh, the doll may have an apish look. Sometimes, because of sock size, the arms will be on the short side, but that is part of the folkish charm of the medium.

Directions for this project begin on page 42.

24

Pocket Pal

WHAT CHILD COULD RESIST THESE SIMPLE, ENDEARING CHARACTERS? YOU CAN MAKE A POCKET PAL IN LESS THAN AN HOUR, CREATE AN ENTIRE PLAY FAMILY IN HALF A DAY, AND MAKE MINIATURE VERSIONS TO TUCK INTO POCKETS OR BACKPACKS. IT'S A GOOD PROJECT FOR USING UP LEFTOVER PARTS OF SOCKS, TOO.

SOCKS

1 colored sport sock for the body
1 sock of the same size for the head

NOTIONS

Matching thread
Stuffing
Ribbon
Embroidery floss or paint for face

Head and Body

ONE Stuff the toe of the sock intended for the head. Pocket Pal can have a cheeky, child-shaped head or a simple round one. Prepare the head and neck according to the basic instructions (fig. a) and set aside.

TWO Cutting straight across just below the heel, remove the foot of the colored sock (fig. b). Stuff the toe section. (The toe seam can run across the front of the doll to denote feet.) Continue stuffing so that the doll has some firmness but not so much that you will have a hard time stitching through the body.

figure a

THREE Run a gathering thread around the top. Seat the head, then pull the gathering up, tucking the seam allowance to the inside. Ladder stitch the head to the body.

FOUR With matching thread and using a stabbing running stitch, sew the lines to denote arms and legs. Turn the doll to check both back and front stitch placements during this process.

Hat and Face

ONE Remove the upper part of the colored sock from the heel by cutting straight across (fig. b). Run a gathering stitch around the cut edge of the upper. Draw the gathering up, turning the seam allowance in. Overcast the outside of the opening to make the top of the hat, then knot off. Pull the hat onto the doll's head. Turn up a cuff. Overcast the hat to the doll's head along the fold.

TWO Paint or embroider the face.

Finishing Touches

Tie a ribbon around the neck.

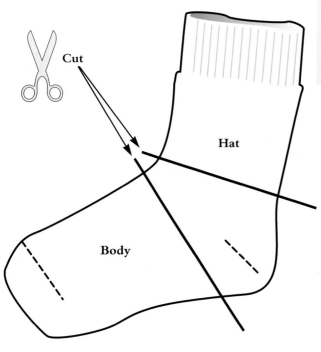

figure b

Patriotic Pals

READY FOR THE FOURTH OF JULY PICNIC
AT THE BEACH, THESE RED–WHITE–AND–
BLUE VERSIONS OF THE POCKET PAL MAY
INSPIRE YOU TO YOUR OWN VARIATIONS
ON THAT SIMPLE DESIGN.

Patriotic Pals

SOCK TIP:

Use the directions for the basic Pocket Pal, along with the notions listed here.

NOTIONS

10" (25.5 cm) of pregathered eyelet lace

18" (46 cm) of ribbon

Embroidery floss for shoelaces

Hat

ONE Cut a piece of eyelet long enough to go around the head at the hairline plus $\frac{1}{2}$" (1.5 cm). Pin the eyelet to the doll's head and sew, turning under $\frac{1}{4}$" (1 cm) of both cut ends at the back. (Use an overcast stitch and work along the edge of the casing where it is stitched to the lace, either from the top of the lace or from the underside with the lace held up.)

TWO Free the upper of the body sock by cutting straight across. Pull this piece onto the head, cut edge first. As you adjust the upper over the lace casing, turn under a narrow seam allowance to the inside.

THREE Smooth the sock up to the crown. Mark the crown with pins. Remove the hat and trim the top to within $\frac{1}{4}$" (1 cm) of the pins. Run a gathering thread around the opening and pull it up, tucking the seam allowance inside. Overcast the gathered area before knotting off. Pull the hat back into place on the head and overcast it to the lace. Tack a bow onto the side of the hat.

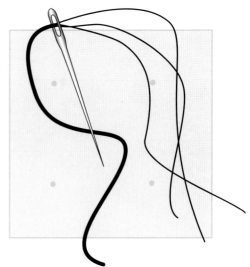

ONE *For the shoelaces, thread a needle with three strands of embroidery floss. Imagine four dots arranged at the corners of a square on one foot, or place pins as markers.*

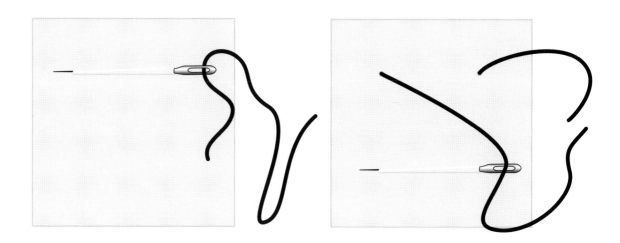

TWO *Insert the needle at the upper right dot and bring it out at the upper left. Leave three or four inches of embroidery floss extending from the first dot.*

THREE *Insert the needle at the lower right dot, bring it out at the lower left, and pull the thread up.*

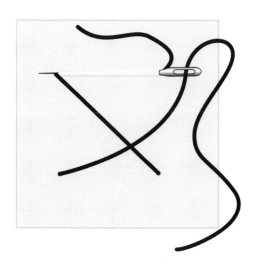

FOUR *Insert the needle again at the upper right, exiting at the upper left. Leave three or four inches of floss extending from the upper left corner.*

FIVE *Tie the two loose strands of embroidery floss in a bow and trim the ends. Repeat with the other foot.*

Cradle Baby

PERFECT FOR A BABY'S FIRST SOCK DOLL,
CRADLE BABY CAN BE A SIMPLE STUFFED
TOY OR AN ATTENTION-GETTING RATTLE.
YOU MIGHT SEW SEVERAL TO A LONG
GROSGRAIN RIBBON AND TIE IT IN A SPOT
WHERE THE BABY CAN TOUCH THEM, AND
EVEN VARY THE MATERIALS IN EACH RATTLE
TO GET DIFFERENT SOUNDS. WITHOUT THE
RATTLE, THE DOLL MAKES A GOOD SEWING
PROJECT FOR AN OLDER CHILD READY TO
LEARN SEVERAL DIFFERENT STITCHES.

SOCKS

1 sock for the head, size 4

1 colored sock for the body and cap, size 4

NOTIONS AND TOOLS

Matching thread

Stuffing

12" (31 cm) of lace or wide ribbon

18" (46 cm) of narrow ribbon

Plastic film canister (the small white ones work best) or pill bottle with lid

A few beans or pieces of macaroni

Hot-glue gun

Embroidery floss or paint for face

Rattle

Place the beans or macaroni in the film canister. Run a thin line of hot glue around the inside rim of the cap, then press the cap onto the canister. Run another line of hot glue around the outside where the cap joins the cylinder, to seal it. Set it aside to dry.

Head and Body

O N E   Stuff the toe of the head sock and model a child-shaped head (fig. a). Prepare the head and neck according to the basic instructions. Set aside.

T W O   Make a straight cut just below the heel on the colored sock to remove the foot (fig. b). Pad the toe with a large piece of stuffing. Wrap the rattle in stuffing and insert it, then continue to stuff all the way around the rattle and on top of it.

figure a

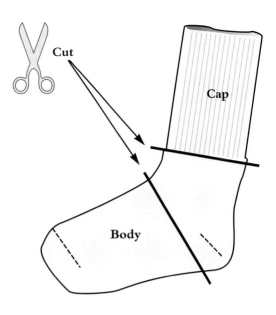

figure b

T H R E E   Run a gathering stitch around the top of the body. Seat the head and pull the gathering stitches up, tucking the seam allowance to the inside. Ladder stitch the head to the body.

Cap and Face

O N E   Cut straight across the colored sock at the base of the ribbing (fig. b). Pull the finished end of the ribbing down over the doll's head, wrong side out (if there is a wrong side). Turn up a narrow cuff and adjust the hat on the head.

T W O   Thread a needle with thread that matches the cap. Pinch the extra fabric in at the crown, then remove the cap. Run a gathering stitch around the pinched area, pull the gathering up, and knot off. Trim the excess fabric. Turn the cap right side out and fit it onto the head, then overcast it in place.

T H R E E   Paint or embroider the face.

Finishing Touches

Cut a piece of lace or wide ribbon long enough to go around the neck one and a half times. Run a gathering stitch along one edge, then draw it up at the neck to form a ruffle and tack it to the doll. Tie a narrow ribbon around the neck and finish with a bow. Tack the ribbon securely to the doll.

Terry

THE TODDLER'S TODDLER, TERRY MAKES
AN ESPECIALLY SOFT AND CUDDLY BED-
TIME FRIEND. OF THE DOLLS WITH LEGS,
TERRY IS THE EASIEST TO MAKE AND
REQUIRES ONLY ONE SOCK FOR THE BODY.
THE INSIDE OF THE SOCK PROVIDES THE
TERRY TEXTURE HERE, A REMINDER THAT
THE "WRONG" SIDES OF SOCKS CAN PRO-
VIDE INTERESTING PATTERNS AND LOOKS
FOR MANY PROJECTS.

SOCKS

1 sock for the head and hands, size 9–11

1 terry-lined sock for the body, size 9–11

NOTIONS

Matching thread

Stuffing

10" (26 cm) of pregathered eyelet lace

Ribbon for two bows

Embroidery floss or paint for face

Head, Body, and Legs

O N E Stuff the toe of the sock to be used for
the head and model a child-shaped head.
Prepare the head and neck according to the
basic instructions (fig. a). Set the head aside.

figure a

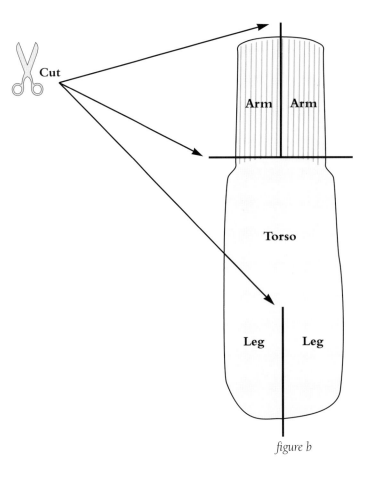

Arm | Arm

Torso

Leg | Leg

figure b

TWO Lay the body sock so that the instep faces up and the heel is centered and out of sight (fig. b). Cut straight across to remove the top third of the sock. Cut this top piece lengthwise down the center for the arms; set the arm pieces aside.

THREE For the body and legs, make a lengthwise cut up the center of the foot, from the toe to about midpoint (fig. b). With the smooth side out, ladder stitch a seam that will round one foot, continue up the leg, cross the crotch, move down the other leg, and round the other foot (fig. c). Turn terry side out.

FOUR Stuff the feet. Weave a straight pin across the top of each foot (fig. d). Finish stuffing the legs and body.

FIVE Run a gathering stitch around the top and seat the head (see "Starting Out"). Draw up the neck, pushing the cut edges to the inside. Attach the head to the body with a ladder stitch. Bend the feet forward and ladder stitch across them twice to hold them in position.

Hands and Arms

ONE For the hands, cut two 1¾ x 2" (4.5 x 5 cm) pieces from the leftover head sock or a scrap piece. Stretch should be across the longest side.

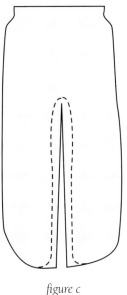

figure c

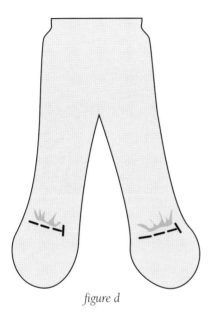

figure d

neck. Turn the cut edges of the lace under at the back and overcast them together. Sew a small ribbon bow on the front.

T W O Paint or embroider features and hair. Sew a bow on top of the head, if you wish.

figure e

T W O Fold one piece in half with right sides together to make a 1 x 1¾" (2.5 x 4.5 cm) rectangle. Make a narrow seam up the side opposite the fold. Run a gathering stitch around one open end. Pull up the gathering and knot off. Turn right side out and stuff. Repeat with the other hand (fig. e).

T H R E E Fold the arm pieces with terry sides together. Backstitch the long edge of one. Turn the arm right side out and run a gathering stitch around the finished end. Insert the hand and draw up the gathering. Ladder stitch the hand firmly to the arm. Repeat with the other arm.

F O U R Stuff both arms. Turn in the upper edges of the arms and overcast them to the body.

Ruffle and Face

Note: *If you intend the doll for a very young child, either omit the small bows in these steps or sew them on very firmly.*

O N E Cut a piece of eyelet lace that will go around the doll's neck about one and one-half times. Run a gathering stitch along the casing of the lace. Draw the lace up until it fits the doll's

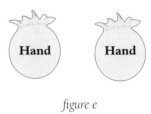

SOCK TIP:

These terry sport socks have a single-fold cuff. A six-pack of socks with three pairs each of face/hand socks and body socks makes six dolls. Use leftovers for heads for dolls with hats and hair.

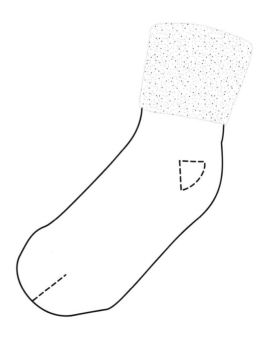

Poppy

WHAT CHILD MOTHER OR CHILD FATHER
COULD RESIST THIS BABY? POPPY IS
EQUALLY STYLISH MADE WITH A DELICATELY
PATTERNED SOCK THAT LOOKS LIKE FINE
HAND KNITTING, AS HERE, OR WITH
ANKLETS OR CREW SOCKS.

 **SOCK TIP:**

>   The uppers of the socks used for the
>   body should be at least as long as the
>   feet.

SOCKS

   1 pair for the body, size 9–11

   1 sock for the head, size 9–11

NOTIONS

   Matching thread

   Stuffing

   24" (62 cm) of ribbon for bonnet ties

   Two small buttons for drop-seat flap (optional)

   Embroidery floss or paint for face

Head, Legs, and Body

   O N E Stuff the toe of the head sock and model
   a child-shaped head. Prepare the head and neck
   according to the basic instructions and set aside
   (fig. a).

   T W O Fold up the toe of one body sock. With
   the toe still folded, fold the foot of the sock
   over the upper with the middle of the heel at
   the fold line. Cut straight across the upper
   where the toe fold lands (fig. b). (This piece,
   including the foot and the upper, will form the
   legs and torso.)

figure a

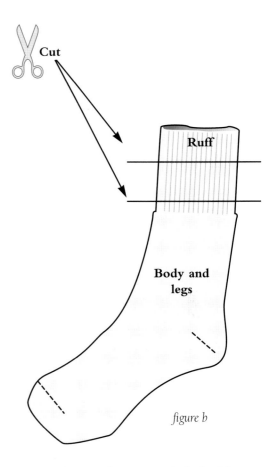

figure b

T H R E E Arrange this piece with the heel facing up and the instep centered and out of sight.
Fold the heel toward the upper. Cut up the center of the sock from the toe almost to the heel
(fig. c).

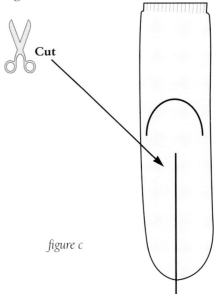

figure c

figure d

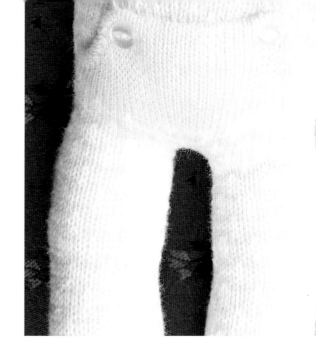

FOUR To make a fake drop seat, stitch a small button securely onto the top of each side of the folded-up heel (fig. d). Stitch through two thicknesses of heel and one of upper, being careful not to catch the other side of the upper. (**Note:** *For children under three, the heel can either be overcast in place without the buttons or left unfolded.*)

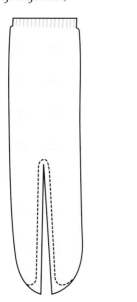

figure e

FIVE Turn the sock inside out and backstitch up the leg seams, rounding the feet (fig. e). Trim the corners of the feet. Turn right side out. Stuff the feet. Weave a straight pin across the top of each foot. Continue to stuff the legs and body. Check body proportion and trim if necessary.

SIX Run a gathering stitch around the open end. Seat the head and draw the gathering up, pushing the cut edge to the inside. Sew the head to the body with a ladder stitch.

SEVEN Remove the pins and bend the feet forward. Ladder stitch the feet in place, going across each one twice.

Hands and Arms

ONE For the hands, cut two pieces $1\frac{3}{4}$ x 2" (4.5 x 5 cm) from the sock used for the head. Stretch should go across the long side. Fold each piece in half with right sides together to form a $1\frac{3}{4}$ x 1" (4.5 x 2.5 cm) rectangle.

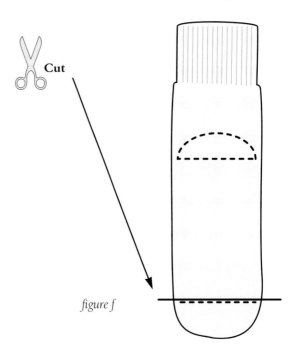

Cut

figure f

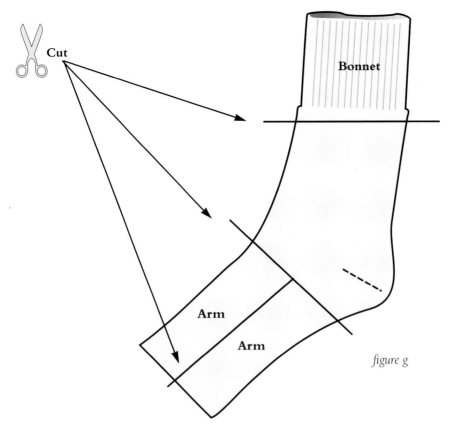

Cut

Bonnet

Arm

Arm

figure g

TWO On one hand, backstitch a narrow seam along the side opposite the fold. Run a gathering stitch around one open end and draw it up. Turn right side out and stuff. Repeat with the other hand.

THREE For the arms, fold the second body sock so that the instep is facing up and the heel is centered out of sight. Cut straight across to remove the toe (fig. f). Refold the sock so the heel is to one side and cut straight across just below the heel (fig. g). Cut this tube lengthwise down the center.

FOUR Fold each arm piece right sides together. Backstitch along the long side of one piece. Turn right side out. Run a gathering stitch around one end and insert one hand. Draw up the gathering, pushing the seam allowance to the inside. Ladder stitch the hand to the arm. Repeat with the other arm.

FIVE Check both arms for length and trim them if necessary. Turn the upper edges of the arms in and overcast them to the body.

Ruff, Bonnet, and Face

ONE For the neck ruff, measure down 1¼" (3.5 cm) from the finished edge of the leftover ribbing for the body sock. Cut straight across (fig. b). Run a gathering stitch around the cut edge of the ruff and pull it over the head. Draw the gathering up while pushing the cut edge under the ruff. Ladder stitch the ruff to the head. Overcast the outer edge of the ruff to the body.

TWO For the bonnet, measure from the edge of the face to the center back of the head. Add ¼" (1 cm) to this measurement. Use this figure to measure down from the finished upper edge of the sock used for the arms and make a straight cut across the sock (fig. g). Cut lengthwise through a single thickness to open this tube.

THREE Run a gathering thread along the edge opposite the finished edge. Draw it up and knot off. Pull the bonnet onto the head, stretching it into place and tucking the cut edges under. Pin the bonnet in place and overcast it to the head along the front and lower edges.

FOUR Paint or embroider the face.

Finishing Touches

Sew ribbons to each side of the bonnet and tie them in a bow under the chin.

Emily

SWEET-FACED EMILY CAN DO MORE THAN
CUDDLE A BABY—SHE'S ALSO GREAT FOR
CARRYING SMALL GREETING CARDS TO
FRIENDS OR FOR PRESENTING A CHILD
WITH A BAG OF TINY TREATS. THIS IS A
GOOD PROJECT TO SHOWCASE A SPECIAL
SOCK WITH TINY FLOWERS, DOTS, OR
STRIPES KNITTED INTO IT.

SOCK TIP:

The upper of the sock for the body
should be at least half as long as the
sock foot.

SOCKS

1 sock for the head, size 7–8½

1 sock for the body, size 7–8½

NOTIONS

Matching thread

Stuffing

1 oz. (28 grams) of yarn for hair (baby-weight,
in the photo)

Hair loom (see page 15)

Wide-toothed comb

18" (46 cm) of ribbon for pigtails

Lace or other trim for neck

A pair of doll socks or knit fabric for Emily's
doll (optional)

Embroidery floss or paint for face

figure a

Head and Body

ONE Stuff the toe of the sock intended for the
head (Emily has a childlike profile). Prepare the
head and neck according to the basic instructions (fig. a). Set the head aside.

TWO Remove the foot from the body sock by
cutting straight across just below the heel (fig.
b). Stuff the toe. (The toe seam can run across
the front of the doll to denote feet.) Continue
stuffing, giving the doll some firmness but not
so much that stitching through the body will be
difficult.

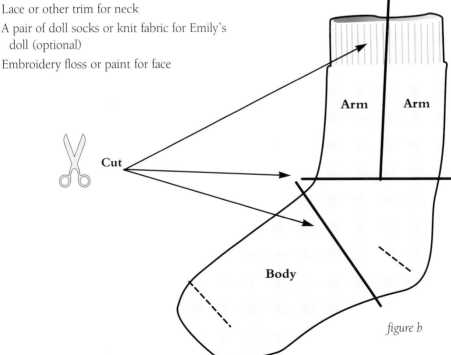

Arm   Arm

Cut

Body

figure b

THREE Run a gathering stitch around the top. Seat the head, then pull the gathering up, tucking the seam allowance to the inside. Ladder stitch the head to the body and knot off.

FOUR With matching thread, denote the legs by stab stitching from the toe to about midpoint on the body.

Hands

ONE From the leftover head sock, cut two pieces 1½ x 2" (4 x 5 cm) for the hands. Be sure the stretch is across the long side.

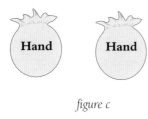

figure c

TWO Fold one piece in half with right sides together to form a rectangle 1 x 1½" (2.5 x 4 cm). Backstitch a narrow seam along the side opposite the fold. Run a gathering stitch around one open end, draw it up, and knot off. Turn the hand right side out and stuff. Repeat for the other hand. Set the hands aside (fig. c).

Arms

ONE Trim the heel away from the body sock with a straight cut across. From the raw edge, cut up the center of the upper through both thicknesses, to the finished edge (fig. b). (These are the arms.)

TWO Fold one arm piece with right sides together and pin. Backstitch the side opposite the fold, then turn right side out. Pinning as needed, position one hand inside the ribbed end of one arm and overcast it firmly in place. Repeat with the other arm and hand.

THREE Before you sew the arms to the body at the neck, adjust them for length by turning excess fabric to the inside or by trimming. Stuff each arm loosely.

FOUR Overcast across the open end of one arm, then ladder stitch it to the neck and knot off. Repeat for the other arm. Tack the hands together. Backstitch a length of lace or trim around the neck.

Hair and Face

ONE Measure the doll's part from the forehead to the nape of the neck and double this figure to determine how long a hairpiece to weave on the hair loom. Use strands of yarn 9" (23 cm) long to weave the hairpiece (see page 00).

TWO Cut the carpet thread and remove the wig from the loom. Retie the carpet thread, making a closed loop of the woven yarn. Flatten the loop and pin it in place on the doll's part. Overcast the wig to the part, catching both sides of the loop and the head in each stitch (figs. d and e).

THREE Comb the hair to each side with a wide-toothed comb. Gather the pigtails and stitch them to the side of the head (fig. f). Tie a ribbon bow around each one.

FOUR Paint or embroider the face.

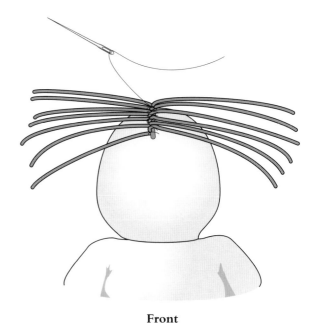

Front

figure d

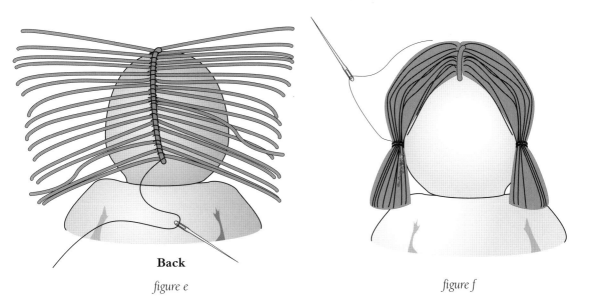

Back

figure e

figure f

Emily's Doll

Emily's doll is made from a pair of doll socks intended for a 12–14" (31–36 cm) child doll. (If you can't find a good pair of these socks, you can make Emily's doll from tubes of knit fabric.)

O N E Work the doll's legs and torso from one sock using the instructions for Poppy (omit the drop seat) (fig. g).

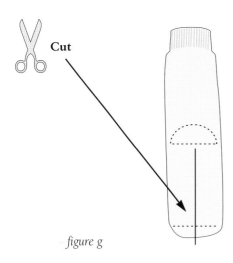

Cut

figure g

T W O Make the head following the directions for one of Emily's hands.

T H R E E For arms and hands, remove the upper of the other sock and cut it down the middle (fig. h). (Each of these pieces is an arm and hand combined.) Fold each piece right

sides together, sew the arm seams, and turn the arms right side out. Gather the finished end of the ribbing on each arm. Stuff both arms.

F O U R For the hands, run a gathering stitch around each wrist, just above the gathered end of each arm. Adjust the arms for length and sew them to the body.

F I V E Make a hat from the foot of the arms sock or, if the uppers of the socks are long enough, make a hat with ribbing from leftover sock fabric above the torso.

S I X Make a few embroidered stitches to suggest a face.

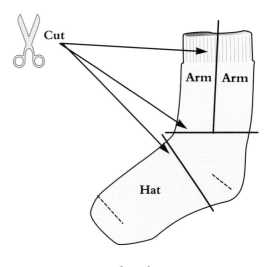

Cut

Arm **Arm**

Hat

figure h

Elizabeth Ann

AS APPEALING AS STRAWBERRY-
MARSHMALLOW ICE CREAM OR
CHERRY AND APPLE BLOSSOMS, THIS
PINK-AND-WHITE CHARMER IS A
DRESSED-UP VARIATION OF POPPY. (USE
THE INSTRUCTIONS FOR POPPY BUT OMIT
THE BONNET.) HER REMOVABLE PINAFORE
IS MADE FROM WIDE EYELET LACE.

SOCK TIP:

Depending on the size of the doll and
the available eyelet, make the pinafore
smock or gown length.

SOCK TIP:

Machine stitching works best for attaching ribbon or pregathered eyelet because
of their tight weaves—see steps 3 and 4.

NOTIONS

Wide eyelet lace—if pregathered, enough to go
1½ times around the doll plus 1" (2.5 cm); if
not pregathered, enough to go twice around
the doll plus 1" (2.5 cm)

Narrow pregathered eyelet for shoulder straps

1 yd. (0.9 m) of ribbon ½" (2 cm) wide for sash

12" (31 cm) of pregathered ribbon for headband

Rosette for headband

Embroidery floss for hair

Pinafore

ONE For eyelet that is not pregathered, trim
the long unfinished edge. On each of the cut
ends, make a ¼" (1 cm) hem and stitch it in
place. Run two gathering threads the length of
the eyelet, ¼" (1 cm) from the unfinished edge
and ⅛" (0.5 cm) from the finished edge. Draw
these up until the skirt fits the doll.

TWO Alternative to step 1: If the eyelet is pregathered, hem the cut ends as in step 1. Run a
gathering stitch along the casing and draw it up
until the skirt fits the doll.

THREE Cut a length of ½" (1.5 cm) wide
ribbon that will go around the doll and tie
in a big bow at the back. Pin the center of
the ribbon to the center of the skirt, covering
the gathering stitches (or casing) with one
edge of the ribbon. Continue pinning out to
both sides of the skirt. Machine stitch or backstitch this edge of the ribbon to the
skirt. Fold the other edge to the inside and
overcast it in place. Leave the ties unstitched.

FOUR Cut two pieces of narrow pregathered
eyelet to go over the shoulders. Machine stitch
or backstitch them in place on the wrong side
of the waistband.

Headband and Hair

ONE Cut a piece of pregathered ribbon equal
to the distance around the head at the hairline
plus about ½" (1.5 cm). Sew the ribbon to the
doll's head, tucking under ¼" (1 cm) on each
side at the back. Tack a purchased rosette to the
hairband.

TWO Embroider daisy-stitch bangs.

Sweater Set

STILL YOUNG ENOUGH TO GET A KICK OUT OF DRESSING ALIKE, THESE TWINS IN THEIR CONTRASTING TURTLENECKS ARE SET FOR THE SANDBOX, A TRIP TO THE ZOO OR THE SKATING RINK, OR A FAMILY REUNION. ALTHOUGH HERE THEIR SWEATERS ARE MADE FROM PATTERNED SOCKS, THEY MAKE A GREAT PROJECT FOR INCORPO-RATING OTHER KINDS OF NEEDLEWORK. TRY SMOCKING THE RIBBING OF CREW SOCKS . . . ON PLAIN SOCKS, CROSS-STITCH DESIGNS IN DUPLICATE STITCH OR APPLIQUÉ PLAYFUL MOTIFS . . . OR EVEN KNIT YOUR OWN SMALL SWEATERS.

SOCK TIP:

Be sure the uppers of the socks for the body and sweater are at least as long as the feet.

SOCKS

1 sock for the body, size 9–11

1 sock for the sweater, size 9–11

1 sock for the head, size 9–11

NOTIONS

Matching thread

Stuffing

1.5 oz. (42 grams) of yarn for long hair

1 oz. (28 grams) of yarn for short hair

Hair loom (see page 15)

Wide-toothed comb

Hot-glue gun (optional)

Ribbon for ponytail

Embroidery floss or paint for faces

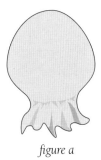

figure a

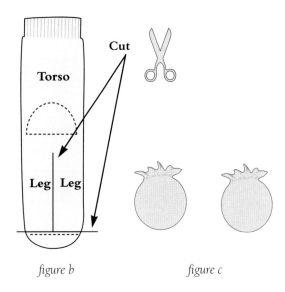

figure b   *figure c*

Note: *The instructions for the head, legs, body, and sweater make one doll.*

Head, Legs, and Body

ONE Stuff the toe of the head sock and model a child-shaped head. Prepare the head and neck according to the basic instructions (fig. a) and set aside.

TWO To make the legs and torso, fold the body sock so that the instep faces up and the heel is centered out of sight (fig. b). Fold the heel toward the upper. Remove the toe with a straight cut just above the seam. Cut up the middle of the sock from the raw edge, almost to the heel. Turn wrong side out. Backstitch up one leg, across the crotch, and down the other leg. Turn right side out.

THREE From a remaining piece of the head sock cut two pieces for feet, each piece 1¾ x 2"

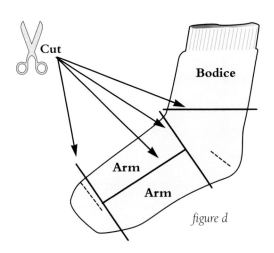

figure d

(4.5 x 5 cm). Stretch should be across the long side. Fold one piece right sides together to form a 1¾ x 1" (4.5 x 2.5 cm) rectangle. Backstitch along the side opposite the fold. Turn right side out.

FOUR Run a gathering stitch around one end. Pull the gathers up, tucking the seam allowance to the inside, and knot off. Stuff this foot. Repeat with the other foot (fig. c).

FIVE Run a gathering stitch around the opening of one leg. Draw the gathering up around

the foot, tucking the seam allowance in. Ladder stitch the foot to the leg. Repeat with the other leg.

SIX Stuff the legs and torso. Check the proportion of the torso to the legs and trim the torso if necessary. Run a gathering stitch around the top. Seat the head. Draw the gathering up, tucking the seam allowance to the inside, and ladder stitch the head to the body.

Sweater and Arms

O N E If the sweater sock has a long upper, measure the doll from neck to waist and add to this measurement enough length to roll the turtleneck and to turn under a small hem at the bottom. Measure this amount down from the top of the sock and make a straight cut across.

T W O Alternative to step 1: If the sweater sock has an upper of ordinary length, remove the upper with a cut straight across and just above the heel (fig. d).

T H R E E Pull the body of the sweater over the doll's head. Arrange the ribbing around the doll's neck to look like a turtleneck. Turn under the cut edge at the waist and overcast the fold to the body.

F O U R For the arms, free the foot tube of the sweater sock by removing the toe and heel (fig. d). Cut lengthwise up the center of this tube through both thicknesses. From a leftover piece of the head sock or a scrap of knit fabric cut two 1¾ x 2" (4.5 x 5 cm) pieces for the hands. Finish as for the feet (fig. c) but use less stuffing.

F I V E Fold one arm right sides together and backstitch up the long side. Turn right side out.

Run a gathering stitch around one end and, turning the seam allowance in, gather the arm around the hand. Ladder stitch the hand to the arm. Repeat with the other arm and hand.

S I X Stuff both arms and check them for length. Turn in the upper edges and overcast them to the body, stitching through the sweater and the body sock.

Ponytail

O N E Measure from a point on the hairline to the crown, add the desired ponytail length, and double this measurement. Cut all the hair strands this length. Measure around the head at the hairline for the length of the wig. Weave the wig on the hair loom (see pages 15–16).

T W O Cut the carpet thread and remove the wig from the loom. Retie the ends of the carpet thread to make a circlet of the woven hair. Pin the circlet in place around the hairline and sew it to the head (fig. e). Pull all the hair to the crown, combing gently with a wide-toothed comb. Run a gathering thread around the ponytail and draw it up (fig. f). Tie with ribbon, if you wish.

T H R E E For curly bangs, wind yarn onto a ruler for several inches. Backstitch the yarn along the edge of the ruler. Pull the yarn off and overcast the stitched edge of the coil in place on the doll's forehead.

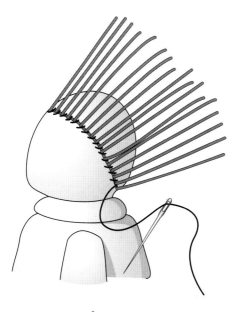

figure e

figure f

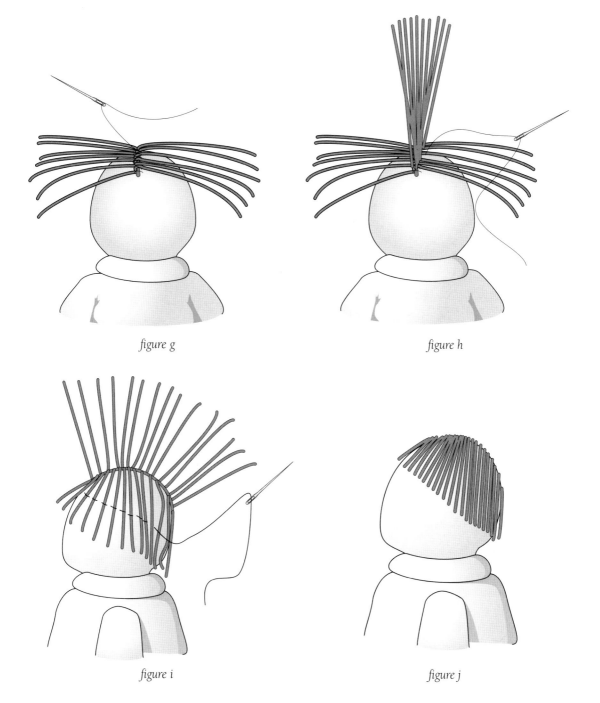

figure g

figure h

figure i

figure j

Short Hair

ONE Measure the length of the part line and double that to get the length of the wig. Measure from the part line to the shoulder and double that for the length of each strand. Weave two wig pieces on the hair loom using these measurements (see pages 15–16).

TWO Tie the ends of the carpet thread of one piece, flatten the circlet, and sew it to the part line (fig. g). Use an overcast stitch and catch both sides as well as the head. Knot the ends of the carpet thread on the second weaving and, holding the first layer up, stitch the second layer just beneath the first (fig. h). Backstitch the under layer around the head at the hairline (fig. i)—for speed, use a hot-glue gun. Comb all the hair down gently with a wide-toothed comb and give the doll a bowl cut or whatever style you choose (fig. j).

Finishing Touches

Paint or embroider the faces.

Beach Buddies

These best friends in their sporty matching outfits seem like go-any-where summertime chums—beach trips, visits to Grandma, birthday par-ties, the county fair. The largest fig-ures in the book, they measure about 17" (44 cm).

SOCK TIP:

All the Beach Buddies socks need uppers as long as the feet. If you can't find smooth-knit socks for their bodies, fine-ribbed socks or knee socks will work.

SOCKS

2 pairs of socks for the bodies, men's size 10–13

2 socks in contrasting colors for the clothes, men's size 13–16

NOTIONS

Matching thread

Stuffing

1 yd. (.9 m) of ribbon for halter straps

1.5 oz. (42 grams) of yarn for hair

Embroidery floss or paint for face

Before you begin: Make a note of the dis-tance from the toe to the heel on one body sock. You'll use this figure to measure the arms. The diagrams and instructions for the head, legs, and body are for one twin, work-ing with one pair of socks.

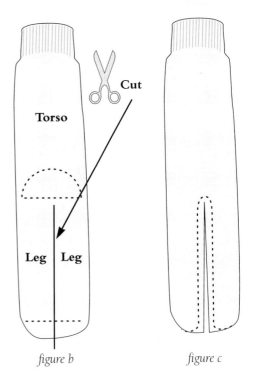

figure b   *figure c*

Head, Legs, and Body

ONE Stuff the toe of one body sock and model a child-shaped head. Prepare the head and neck according to the basic instructions (fig. a). Set aside.

TWO Lay the other body sock so that the instep faces up, with the heel centered under-neath (fig. b). Fold the heel toward the upper. Cut up the center of the foot from the toe almost to the heel. Turn wrong side out.

THREE Sew the leg seam, rounding the first foot, moving up one leg, across the crotch, down the other leg, and rounding the other foot (fig. c). Trim any excess fabric. Turn right side out.

FOUR Stuff the feet. Weave a pin through the fabric above each foot, then stuff the legs. Remove the pins from the feet and ladder stitch each foot to point forward. Stuff the body. Adjust the length of the torso to be more pro-portional to leg length if necessary. Seat the head and ladder stitch it to the body.

figure a

SOCK TIP:

A dowel may make stuffing these long legs easier. The sides need to be smooth, but a rough-sawn end helps control the stuffing material.

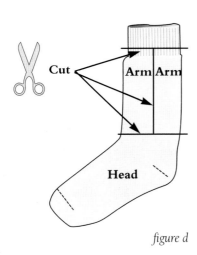

figure d

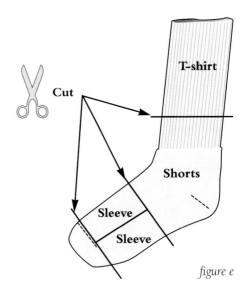

figure e

Arms and Hands

O N E Using the measurement you noted at the beginning of the project, cut a length of tube from the remaining upper (fig. d). Then cut this piece in half lengthwise. (These are the arms and hands.)

T W O Refold one of the pieces so that the right sides are together and make a seam along the side opposite the fold. Turn right side out. Run a gathering stitch around the end where the hand is to be. Draw the gathering thread up, tucking the seam allowance inside. Knot off. Repeat with the other arm. Stuff both arms, adjusting for length if necessary.

T H R E E To make hands, run a gathering stitch around each wrist (about an inch [2.5 cm] from the finished end of the arm), cinch it in, and knot off.

F O U R Set the arms and body aside and make the other buddy with the second pair of body socks.

Shorts

O N E Pull one colored sock on over one body so that the heel covers the doll's rear. To mark for cutting, place a pin at the waist and one where you want the bottom hem of the shorts to fall. Allow at least an extra ¼" (1 cm) at both waist and legs for turning under.

T W O Remove the sock from the body. Make a straight cut across the sock for the waist and another for the bottom of the shorts (fig. e). Now fold the shorts so that the instep faces up and the heel is centered underneath, out of sight. Fold the heel toward the waist. Starting at the cross cut for the legs, cut up the center of

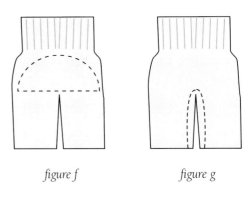

figure f   figure g

the sock through both thicknesses and end your cut just below the heel (fig. f).

T H R E E Turn inside out and sew the leg seams (fig. g). Turn right side out. Pull the shorts onto the doll, turn the cut edges under, and overcast them to the body.

F O U R Repeat steps 1–3 to make shorts for the other doll, using the sock of the contrasting color (fig. h).

T-shirt

O N E Hold a leftover piece of ribbing upside down against the chest of one doll (fig. e). (It's your choice whether to match the t-shirts to the shorts or to use contrasting colors.) Allow the finished edge to fall at the waist. Smooth the fabric along the chest and into the neck. Place a pin ¼" (1 cm) above the neck to mark the cutting line—this includes the seam allowance.

T W O Remove the sock from the doll and cut straight across at the pin. Run a gathering stitch

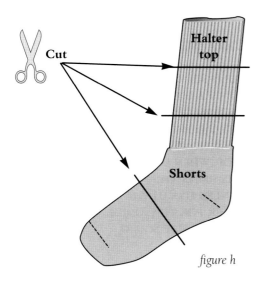

Cut

Halter top

Shorts

figure h

around the cut edge, then pull the piece over the body and draw up the gathering at the neck. Tuck the seam allowance to the inside and ladder stitch the neck of the t-shirt to the doll's neck.

THREE Cut the sleeves from the leftover foot piece that matches the shirt (fig. e). Measure down about 3½" (9 cm) from the cut edge. Cut straight across. To separate the sleeves, cut up the middle of this piece through both thicknesses.

FOUR On one piece, reverse the fold so that the right sides are together. Sew the seam opposite the fold, then turn right side out and pull onto one upper arm. Match the cut upper edges of the arm and the sleeve. Now fold the lower edge of the sleeve under and sew the hem to the arm. Repeat for the other sleeve and arm.

FIVE Sewing through both the arm and the sleeve, run a gathering stitch around the opening of one arm, then pull up the gathering. Overcast the top of the arm to the body, work down one side for about 1" (2.5 cm), ladder stitch under the arm, then overcast again up the other side. Stitching all the way around twice makes the join more firm. Attach the other arm to the body in the same way.

Halter Top

ONE Attach the arms to the other Beach Buddy.

TWO Hold the large leftover piece of ribbing against the doll, positioning the finished edge to form the lower edge of the halter. Mark the top of the halter with a pin, allowing for a ¼" (1 cm) hem.

THREE Remove the sock from the doll and cut straight across the ribbing at the pin (see fig. h). Pull this piece onto the doll's chest with the finished edge at the midriff. Turn under the cut edge at the top.

FOUR Cut one yard of ribbon in quarters. Tack two pieces to the top of the halter, front and back, so that you will be able to tie them into a bow on each shoulder. Tie the bows, then overcast the top of the halter to the doll.

Face and Hair

ONE Paint or embroider the faces. (I find embroidery more effective than paint on dolls with dark skin.)

TWO Make curly hair by following the directions for Merry Anne—if you choose chenille yarn, as in the photo, try the technique in the Sock Tip.

SOCK TIP:

The fibers in chenille yarn are laid out quite differently from those in other yarns and are more prone to twisting and harder to stitch in place. To make curly doll hair with chenille yarn: After winding a coil, pin the working strand to the last round and draw a length of it straight back across the coil.

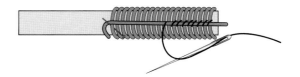

Cut it, leaving a short tail. When backstitching across the coil, carry the thread around this strand as well as each round. Tie a knot at the end, remove the coil, and sew it to the doll's head, again catching the strand that runs perpendicular to each round.

Socko the Clown

A LOOSE-BODIED, GOOD-NATURED CLOWN, SOCKO APPEALS TO THE CHILD IN ALL OF US, AND CREATING THIS DOLL IS A GREAT WAY TO CELEBRATE THE SPONTANEITY, HUMOR, AND FUN CLOWNS REPRESENT. WITH A FEW ALTERATIONS, SOCKO CAN BE LARGE OR SMALL, PASTEL OR BRIGHT, PRINT OR SOLID. AND RESEARCHING CLOWN FACES FOR THIS PROJECT OFFERS A DELIGHTFUL OPPORTUNITY ON ITS OWN.

Socko Junior

HERE IS SOCKO MADE OF SOCKS NOT ONLY OF A DIFFERENT STYLE BUT OF A DIFFERENT SIZE. THE SMALLER A PAIR OF SOCKS, THE SHORTER THE FOOT WILL BE IN PROPORTION TO THE WIDTH. FOR SOCKO JUNIOR, WHEN USING YOUNG CHILDREN'S SOCKS SIMPLY OMIT THE SELF-RUFFLES. YOU MAY NEED TO CUT THE FEET AND HANDS SMALLER FOR THIS JUNIOR VERSION THAN FOR A FULL-SIZE SOCKO.

SOCK TIP:

The uppers of the socks used for the body need to be at least as long as the feet.

SOCKS

2 pairs of smooth-knit sport socks in contrasting colors, size 9–11

1 sock for the head, size 9–11

NOTIONS

Matching thread

Stuffing

18" (46 cm) of ⅞" (2.5 cm) ribbon for ruffle and cockade

Embroidery floss or paint for face

Head

Stuff the toe of the sock intended for the head—Socko's head can be nice and round. Prepare the head and neck according to the basic instructions (fig. a). Set aside.

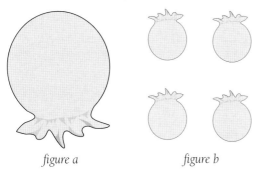

figure a   figure b

Feet and Hands

ONE From the sock for the head, cut four squares 3 x 3" (8 x 8 cm). Lay one square right side up with the stretch going across. Fold it in half, left over right, and stitch a narrow seam along the side opposite the fold.

TWO Run a gathering stitch around one open end, then draw up the stitching and knot off. Turn right side out and stuff (fig. b).

THREE Repeat steps 1 and 2 with the other three pieces. Set the hands and feet aside.

Body and Legs

ONE Cut a slit down the back of one of each pair of contrasting socks to the point of the heel (fig. c). Turn one sock wrong side out and slip the remaining sock, still right side out, into it. Backstitch one continuous seam from cuffs to heels and back up to cuffs. Turn right side out.

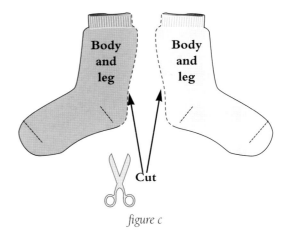

figure c

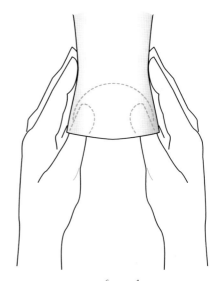

figure d

figure e

TWO To make a ruffle, fold the toe of one sock up inside the foot just far enough that you can sew a gathering stitch through both thicknesses all the way around, ½" (1.5 cm) from the fold (figs. d and e).

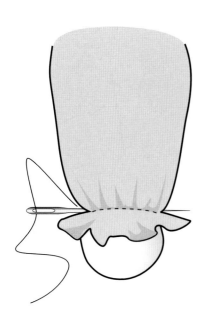

figure f

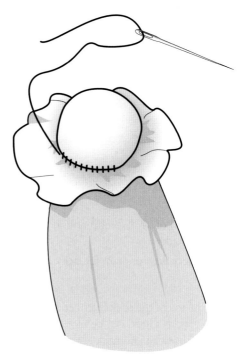

figure h

figure g

THREE Draw the gathering stitch up and tuck the unfinished end of one foot inside. To hold the foot in place, stab stitch through the foot and the gathering several times (fig. f). Push your needle under the ruffle (fig. g) and ladder stitch the foot to the leg gathering (fig. h). Go around twice, then knot off. Repeat steps 2 and 3 with the other leg and foot.

FOUR For a floppy effect, stuff the legs and body only enough to give the doll form. Adjust the length of the torso if necessary, either by trimming it down or by folding excess fabric to the inside. Run a gathering stitch around the top. Seat the head and draw the gathering up. Use a ladder stitch to attach the head firmly all the way around.

Arms

ONE Make a straight cut just above the heel on each of the remaining socks (fig. i). (The sock feet, including the heels, will become the sleeves.) Make the arm ruffles and attach the hands as you did for the legs and feet (figs. d–h). Stuff the arms loosely.

TWO Run a gathering stitch around the top of each arm and draw it up, tucking the seam allowance inside. (The heel will form a puffed sleeve.) Pin the arms to the contrasting sides of the body so that the sleeve looks set-in. Sew the arms to the body using a small overcast stitch and working in a circle around the gathering.

Hat and Face

ONE Make a single cut through one thickness along the side of each remaining upper.. Fold

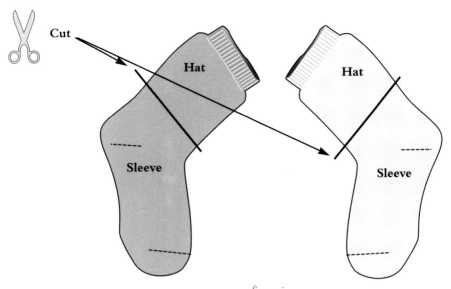

figure i

the ribbing up to the outside (right side) of each piece to make a cuff. Place the two pieces right sides together with the cuffs still folded. Put a pin through all four thicknesses at each side.

TWO At the top of the hat, on each side measure in about one quarter of the overall length across and make a small pencil mark. Lay a ruler against the hat, connecting the side of the hat just above the cuff to a pencil mark at the top (fig. j). Mark the line lightly with a pencil. Repeat on the other side. Cut along both pencil lines to tailor the hat.

THREE Finish pinning both sides and backstitch the seams (fig. k). Run a gathering stitch at the top of the hat, pull it up, and knot off. Turn right side out. Arrange the hat on the head and overcast it in place.

FOUR To make the ruffle, measure off enough ribbon to encircle the neck one and a half times. Run a gathering stitch along one edge of the ribbon, draw it up, and place it around the neck. Finish by folding the ends of the ribbon under and sewing the folds together with an overcast stitch.

FIVE For a cockade, with about 4–5" (10–13 cm) of the remaining ribbon, make a few folds and tack the decoration behind the cuff of the hat.

SIX Paint or embroider the face.

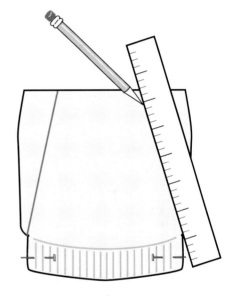

figure j

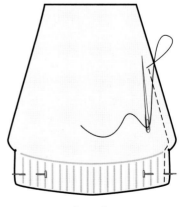

figure k

Patty Patent-Leather

WITH HER WHITE TIGHTS AND SWEATER, DRESS-UP SHOES, AND LONG, LONG HAIR, PATTY MAKES A COMPANION TO THRILL SMALL HEARTS. UNLIKE THE SOCKS FOR MOST OF THE OTHER FIGURES, PATTY'S BODY SOCK IS USED UPSIDE DOWN TO SHOW OFF ITS SUBTLE RIBBING PATTERN, A METHOD THAT ALSO WORKS FOR PEARL.

 ## SOCK TIP:

The socks for the dress must have uppers at least as long as the feet and should not have elastic fibers knitted in. The socks for the body must have uppers the same length or only slightly longer than the feet. If you can't find soft, blousing socks, use the dress instructions for Merry Anne.

SOCKS

1 pair of socks for the body and arms, size 9–11

1 pair of socks that blouse from a narrow cuff for the dress, size 9–11

1 sock for the head, size 9–11

NOTIONS

Matching thread

Stuffing

12" (31 cm) of pregathered eyelet lace

24" (62 cm) of ribbon for bows

1.5 oz. (42 g) of yarn for hair

Hair loom (see page 15)

Hot-glue gun (optional)

Purchased shoes

Embroidery floss or paint for face

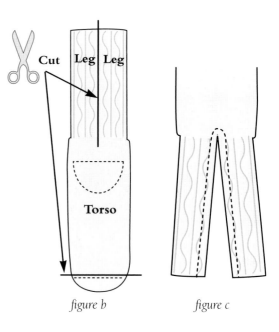

figure b   *figure c*

Head, Body, and Legs

O N E Stuff the toe of the sock intended for the head, modeling a child-shaped head. Prepare the head and neck according to the basic instructions (fig. a). Set aside.

T W O Fold the sock for the body so that the instep faces up and the heel is centered out of sight (fig. b). Remove the toe with a straight cut just above the seam. Fold the heel toward the foot to prevent cutting it. Separate the legs by cutting lengthwise through both thicknesses from the finished edge nearly to the heel.

T H R E E Turn the sock wrong side out. Backstitch up one leg, across the crotch, and down the other leg (fig. c). Turn right side out.

F O U R Run a gathering stitch around the open end of one leg and pull it up just enough to make a flat closure with rounded ends that goes from side to side. Tuck the seam allowance in and overcast across the foot (fig. d). Knot off. Repeat with the other leg.

figure a

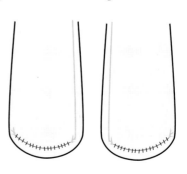

figure d

FIVE Stuff each foot and weave a straight pin across the top of each. Stuff the legs, leaving a space at the top of each to allow it to bend. Stuff the torso. Check the proportion of legs and torso and trim the torso if necessary.

SIX Run a gathering stitch around the top. Seat the head. Pull up the gathering, tucking the seam allowance inside. Attach the head to the body with a ladder stitch.

SEVEN Remove the pins from the feet. Bend one foot forward and ladder stitch twice across to hold it in position. Knot off. Repeat for the other foot.

Bodice and Skirt

ONE Make the bodice and skirt from both uppers and one foot of the blousing pair of socks. For the bodice, remove the toe from one sock with a straight cut just above the seam. Make another cut straight across and just below the heel to free the foot tube (fig. e).

TWO Run a gathering stitch around one end of the foot tube. Pull this section over the doll's chest with the gathering thread at the neck. Pull up the gathers, tucking the seam allowance in, and ladder stitch the bodice to the neck.

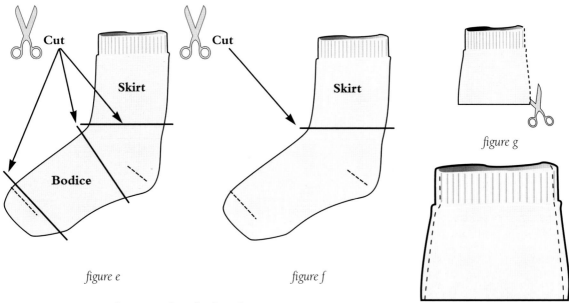

figure e

figure f

figure g

figure h

THREE Cut the uppers from both socks just above the heel (figs. e and f). Make a lengthwise cut through one thickness of each sock upper to open the tubes (fig. g). Lay these two pieces right sides together, ribbing against ribbing, and pin the sides (fig. h). (The ribbing will be the waist.)

FOUR Sew the side seams. Overcast a hem on the lower edge. Pull the skirt onto the doll over the bodice, and overcast the skirt to the bodice.

Arms and Hands

ONE To give the effect of a jumper, cut the arms from the remaining upper of the body socks. (If you prefer the effect of a dress, instead use the remaining foot of the socks used for the skirt.) To make the doll as shown, make a straight cut just above the heel of the leftover body sock (fig. i). Cut this tube in half lengthwise through both thicknesses. Fold each piece right sides together. Backstitch the side seams and turn the arms right side out.

TWO From the leftover piece of sock used for the head, cut two pieces for the hands, each 1¾ x 2" (4.5 x 5 cm). Stretch should be across the long side. Fold each piece right sides together to form a 1 x 1¾" (2.5 x 4.5 cm) rectangle.

THREE Using a backstitch, sew a narrow seam along the side opposite the fold of one piece. Run a gathering stitch around one open end. Draw it up and knot off. Turn right side out and stuff. Repeat with the other hand (fig. j).

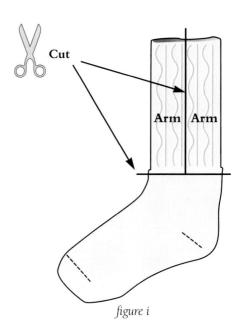

figure i

FOUR Run a gathering stitch around the finished edge of one arm. Place the open end of one hand in the gathered end, pull the gathering up, and ladder stitch the hand to the arm. Repeat with the other arm and hand. Stuff both arms.

FIVE Adjust the length of the arms if necessary. Then turn in the cut edges of the upper arms and overcast the arms to the body, sewing through both the bodice and the body fabric.

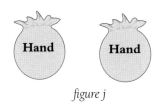

figure j

Ruffle

O N E Cut a piece of pregathered eyelet lace that will go around the doll's neck one and a half times. Run a gathering stitch along the fold of the lace casing. Place the ruffle around the doll's neck and draw it up.

T W O Fold the cut edges of lace under on each side, pin them together, and overcast a small seam. Tack the ruffle to the body at the center back and center front. Make a ribbon bow and tack it to the lace.

Hair and Face

O N E Measure from an imaginary center part line to where you want the ends of the hair to fall and double this measurement. Cut each strand of yarn to this length. To determine the length to weave the wig, measure the length of the part and double it.

T W O For the hair that falls away from the part, make two weavings of the doubled part length on the wig loom (see pages 15–16). Remove the first weaving from the loom and tie the ends of the carpet thread together. Flatten this loop of yarn hair and center it on the head (fig. k). Overcast it in place, catching the head and both sides of the loop. Knot off.

T H R E E Holding the first layer of hair out of the way, overcast the second loop just underneath (fig. l). Using a backstitch or a hot-glue gun, attach the under layer of hair to the head where a natural hairline would be (fig. m). Smooth both layers down and trim the ends.

F O U R For the hair that is drawn back from the temples, measure from the temple to the center back of the head and then to the hair ends. Double this measurement. Cut twelve strands of yarn this length. Fold six strands in half and sew the center fold of these strands to one temple. Repeat for the other temple. Catch all twelve strands up in a ribbon at the back of the head.

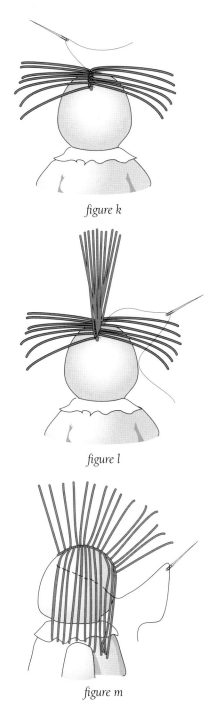

figure k

figure l

figure m

F I V E For curly bangs, wind yarn onto a ruler for several inches. Backstitch the yarn along the edge of the ruler. Pull the yarn off and overcast the stitched edge of the coil in place on the doll's forehead.

S I X Paint or embroider the face.

Finishing Touches

See the list of suppliers at the back of the book for sources of shoes.

Fergus the Fisherman

FERGUS'S SWEATER MARKS HIM AS AN ARAN ISLANDER, AND HIS BEARD, BOOTS, AND WOOL-LOOK TROUSERS EVOKE VISIONS OF FISHING BOATS AND EVENINGS WITH HIS PIPE IN FRONT OF A TURF FIRE. THIS VISION CAPITALIZES ON AN EXCITING BIT OF FASHION NEWS FOR SOCK-DOLL MAKERS: THE PATTERNS KNITTED INTO SOCKS OFTEN REFLECT THE FOLK DESIGNS OF SWEATERS. SEVERAL OTHER PROJECTS ADAPT THIS BASIC DOLL FIGURE: HEIDI THE DOWNHILL SKIER, SANTA, AND THE AUBURN FAMILY FATHER.

SOCK TIP:

You can find wool look-alike socks in less expensive synthetic blends. Be sure the socks for the body and sweater have uppers at least as long as the feet. (The design on the instep of the sweater socks does not have to go all the way around the feet.)

SOCKS

1 gray or brown heather sock for the body, size 9–11

1 pair of cabled or Aran-style socks, size 9–11

1 sock for the head, size 5–6½

NOTIONS

Matching thread

Stuffing

1.5 oz. (42 grams) of yarn for hair and beard

Black felt or thin leather for boots

Embroidery floss or paint for face

figure a

Head, Legs, and Body

ONE Stuff the toe of the sock intended for the head, modeling an adult-shaped head. Prepare the head and neck according to the basic instructions, and set aside (fig. a).

TWO Fold the heather sock so that the instep faces up and the heel is out of sight (fig. b). Cut just above the toe seam to remove the toe. Reach underneath and fold the heel toward the upper to prevent cutting it. Cut up the center of the foot from the raw edge through both thicknesses, nearly to the heel.

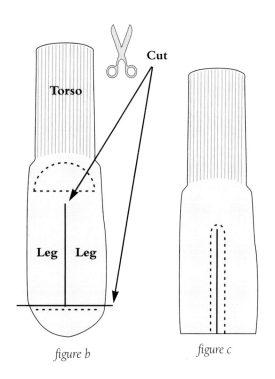

figure b

figure c

THREE Turn the sock wrong side out and backstitch up one leg, across the crotch, and down the other leg (fig. c). Knot off. Turn right side out. Measure up 1½" (4 cm) on one leg

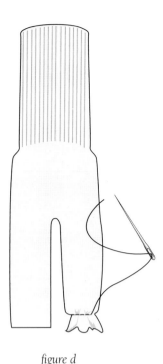

figure d

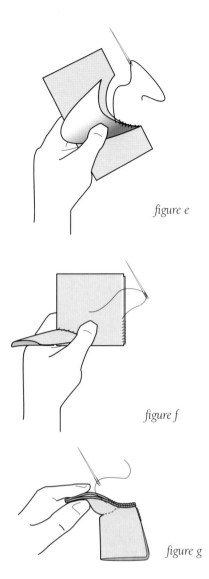

figure e

figure f

figure g

and run a gathering thread around the leg at that measurement (fig. d). Pull it up and knot off. Repeat with the other leg. Stuff the legs and torso.

FOUR Trim the torso, if necessary. Run a gathering stitch around the opening and seat the head. Pull up the gathering, tucking the seam allowance inside. Attach the head to the body with a ladder stitch.

Boots and Feet

ONE Trace and cut out the three pattern pieces for the boots on page 69. Pin them onto black felt or hold them against black leather. Cut two of each piece.

TWO Using an overcast stitch, attach line AB of one instep to line AB of one upper (fig. e). Pull points C and D back away from the toe and tack them together, then sew a short distance up the back of the upper (fig. f). Place points CD of sole against points CD of the upper. Overcast the sole to the upper and the instep, easing the instep in so that points E on the instep and sole meet (fig. g). Continue around to points CD. Knot off.

THREE Stuff the boot. Place the boot around the unstuffed portion of the leg, adding enough fill to stiffen the boot. Overcast up the back of the boot upper. Sew the boot to the leg by overcasting the boot upper to the

stuffed part of the leg, allowing the stuffed fabric to blouse over the boot top. Repeat this process for the other boot.

Sweater

ONE Cut the upper from one patterned sock just above the heel (fig. h). Pull the piece over the doll's head, ribbing first. Arrange the ribbing at the waist. Place a pin in the sweater fabric to mark the neck. Remove the sweater bodice.

TWO Measure an extra $1\frac{1}{4}$ " (3.5 cm) beyond the pin to allow for the turtleneck. Trim away any excess fabric. Turn the cut edge under $\frac{3}{4}$" (2 cm) and to the inside. Run a gathering stitch $\frac{1}{2}$" (1.5 cm) down from the fold, all the way around and through both thicknesses. Pull the bodice back onto the doll, draw the gathering thread up, and knot off.

(Continued on page 68)

Erik

For this variation of Fergus the Fisherman, use the cutting diagram from the Sweater Set to make this Scandinavian's sweater. Otherwise, follow the instructions for Fergus. Don't forget to think of friends with lost-sock problems, recycled-clothing stores, and even laundromats as sources of unique socks. (Erik's sweater came from one of these.)

SOCK TIP:

I like the upper edges of Fergus's arms to lie flat and be placed close to his neck to give the effect of raglan sleeves, but they can also be gathered lightly and placed lower to give the appearance of set-in sleeves.

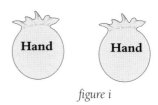

figure i

Hands and Arms

O N E For the hands, cut two rectangles from the remainder of the sock used for the head, 2 x 1½" (5 x 4 cm) each, with the stretch across the long side.

T W O Fold one piece in half, right sides together, to form a rectangle 1 x 1½ inches (2.5 x 4 cm). Sew a narrow seam along the side opposite the fold. Run a gathering stitch around one end. Pull the gathering up and knot off. Repeat for the other hand. Stuff both hands (fig. i).

T H R E E For the arms, cut the upper from the second patterned sock just above the heel (fig. j). Cut lengthwise up the center of this piece from the cut edge to the finished edge, through both thicknesses.

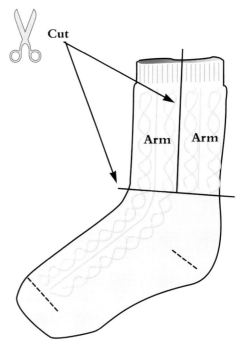

figure j

F O U R Fold cuffs up on the outside. With the cuff still folded, fold one arm lengthwise with right sides together. Backstitch the length opposite the fold. Turn right side out. Run a gathering stitch around the cuff at the fold. Insert the unfinished edge of the hand. Draw up the gathering thread and ladder stitch the hand to the cuff. Repeat for the other arm and hand.

F I V E Stuff the arms. Trim the upper arms if necessary to make arm length proportional to the body. Fold under the upper edge of one arm to the inside and sew the arm to the body as follows: first, overcast across the top, catching both sides of the arm opening and both sweater and body fabric in each stich. Overcast about 1" (2.5 cm) down on one side of the arm, ladder stitch under the arm, then overcast up the other side. Going around twice makes a stronger attachment. Repeat for the other arm.

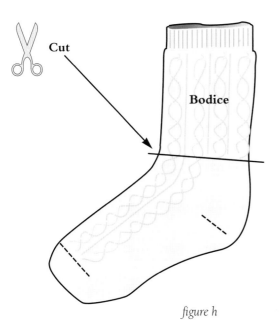

figure h

Patterns

(actual size)

Face, Beard, Hair, and Eyebrows

O N E Paint or embroider the face.

T W O For the beard, wrap yarn around a $\frac{7}{16}$" (1.5 cm) dowel until you have covered a length of the dowel that matches the distance from ear to ear, allowing for a curve just under the mouth. With the yarn still on the dowel, backstitch along one edge the length of the wrapping.

T H R E E Remove the yarn from the dowel without twisting the coil. Lay it in position against the face under the mouth. You may want to pin it in place before you sew. Overcast the coil to the face, catching yarn and thread along the backstitching. Make a slightly shorter coil and apply this about $\frac{1}{4}$" (1 cm) below the first row.

F O U R For the mustache, make another coil to go straight across the face and under the nose. Hold this coil flat against the face and backstitch through all thicknesses along the top and close to the backstitching on the coil. Trim the mustache.

F I V E For hair, on a slightly larger dowel make and apply more coils from ear to ear across the top of the head and across the nape of the neck. Continue making and applying coils to fill in the crown and the back of the head.

S I X To make eyebrows, thread a tapestry needle with 12" (31 cm) of yarn. Insert the needle at the top of the head and bring it out at the outside edge of one eyebrow. Make a single stitch, inserting the needle at the inside edge of the eyebrow and bringing it back out at the outside edge of the eyebrow. Make a tiny stitch, placing the point of the needle next to where it last exited, and push the needle to the top of the head again. Repeat for the other eyebrow.

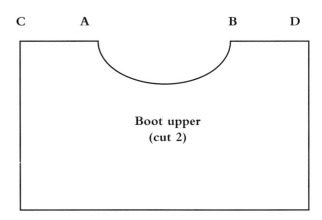

C   A   B   D

Boot upper (cut 2)

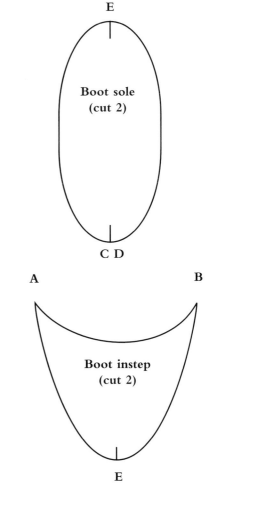

E

Boot sole (cut 2)

C D

A   B

Boot instep (cut 2)

E

Santa

WITH MATCHING SWEATER AND STOCKING CAP, THIS SANTA CUTS A PARTICULARLY DAPPER FIGURE. IF HE'S INTENDED AS A GIFT, YOU MAY WANT TO STUFF HIS BAG WITH SMALL PRESENTS AND CANDY. THE INSTRUCTIONS TAKE THE FISHERMAN DESIGN A STEP FURTHER BY CUTTING THE SWEATER TO ACCOMMODATE A LITTLE ROUND BELLY.

SOCK TIP:

The sweater socks and the body sock need to have uppers at least as long as the feet. For Santa's sweater, use socks whose pattern goes all the way around the feet or that are smooth knit all the way around the feet. Look for the small gold rings for Santa's pack in the jewelry supplies section of a crafts store.

SOCKS

1 red sock for the body, size 9–11

1 pair of red socks in a patterned knit for the sweater, size 9–11

1 sock for the head, size 5–6½

1 sock for Santa's pack, size 9–11

NOTIONS

Matching thread

Stuffing

Cream-colored yarn for beard, mustache, and eyebrows

Red felt for mittens

Black felt or thin leather for boots

Rolled velvet or narrow strips of fur for trim

Pom-pom for hat

Embroidery floss or paint for face

Cardboard for beard loom

6 small gold rings for Santa's pack

Embroidery floss for pack drawstring

Head, Body, and Legs

ONE Stuff the toe of the sock designated for the head—Santa should have a slightly over-

figure a

stuffed, egg-shaped head. Prepare the head and neck according to the basic instructions (fig. a). Set aside.

TWO One sock with a plain knit foot will form the torso and legs. Fold the sock so that the instep faces up and the heel is out of sight (fig. b). Remove the toe by cutting straight across just above the toe seam. Fold the heel toward the upper to prevent cutting it. Cut up the middle of the foot from the cross cut near the toe, almost to the heel.

THREE Turn the sock wrong side out. Backstitch up one leg, across the crotch, and

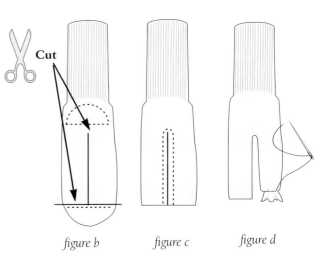

figure b   *figure c*   *figure d*

down the other leg (fig. c). Turn right side out. Measure up 1½" (4 cm) on one leg. Run a gathering stitch around the leg at that point, pull it up, and knot off (fig. d). Repeat with the other leg. Stuff the legs and then the torso.

FOUR For the boots, use the Fergus the Fisherman pattern and instructions. Stitch white trim around the top of each boot after you have sewn it to the leg.

FIVE Trim the torso if necessary for better proportion with the legs. Run a gathering stitch at the top and seat the head. Pull up the gathering, tucking the seam allowance to the inside. Attach the head to the body with a ladder stitch.

Sweater

ONE Remove the uppers of both patterned socks with straight cuts just above the heels (figs. e and f). Make a single cut through a single thickness up the side of each tube. If there is a wide enough cuff, fold it up and to the outside on both pieces. Pin it in place.

TWO Lay the two pieces with right sides together. Pin the side seams. Hold the body of the sweater against the doll's torso with the cuff below the waist. Allowing for a seam allowance to be turned in at the neck, trim away any excess length.

THREE Backstitch both side seams. Turn right side out. Run a gathering stitch around the top. Pull the body of the sweater over Santa's head, ribbing first. Draw up the gathering thread, tucking the seam allowance to the inside, and knot off. Position extra stuffing under the sweater to fill Santa's belly. Overcast the ribbing to the body.

Arms and Mittens

ONE Free the foot tube of one of the sweater socks by making one cross cut just above the toe seam and another just below the heel (fig. e). Make a single lengthwise cut up the middle of this tube, through both thicknesses.

TWO Reverse the fold on each of these pieces so that the right sides are together. Backstitch the long side of one arm, gather the end, pull it up tightly, and knot off. Turn right side out. Repeat with the other arm. Stuff both arms.

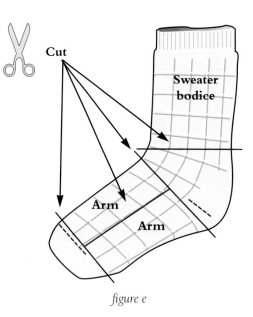

figure e

THREE Trace the mitten pattern onto a piece of paper and cut it out. Cut four mitten pieces from red felt. For each mitten, pin two felt pieces together and sew around the edges with a small overcast stitch. Stuff the thumbs, then the finger areas.

FOUR Push one mitten onto one arm with the thumb positioned so that it turns slightly toward the body. Pin the mitten in place and overcast the upper edge to the arm. Repeat with the other arm and mitten. Sew white velvet or fur trim around the upper edges of the mittens.

FIVE Check the arms for length and trim them if necessary. Run a gathering stitch around the top of one arm. Pull it up slightly, tucking the seam allowance to the inside. Sew the arm to the body, overcasting across the top and about 1" (2.5 cm) down one side. Ladder stitch under the arm and overcast up the other side. Going around twice makes the connection more firm. Knot off. Repeat with the other arm.

Stocking Hat

ONE With a straight cut just below the heel, free the foot of the other sweater sock (fig. f). Turn it wrong side out and pull it onto the head. Turn the cut edge up about ¾" (2 cm), then tuck ¼" (1 cm) into the first fold. Keeping a finger between Santa's head and his hat to avoid sewing the hat to the head, overcast this hem.

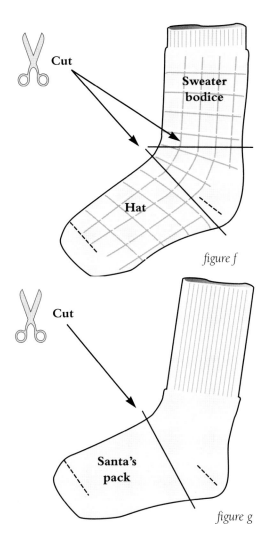

Cut

Sweater bodice

Hat

figure f

Cut

Santa's pack

figure g

T W O   Take the hat off and turn it right side out. Attach the pom-pom to the tip of the hat (the sock toe). Pull the hat back on Santa's head and turn the hem up for a cuff.

Face, Beard, and Eyebrows

O N E   Paint or embroider the face.

T W O   For the beard, measure from below Santa's lip to the point where the end of his beard will fall on his chest. Cut a sturdy piece of cardboard 6" (15 cm) wide, using the beard measurement for length. Wrap the yarn for the beard around this loom until the piece is wide enough to stretch from ear to ear, passing under Santa's lip. Before removing the yarn, backstitch along one edge.

T H R E E   Remove the coil of yarn from the loom. Sew the coil to Santa's face, under the mouth, with an overcast stitch. Trim and shape the beard.

Pattern

(actual size)

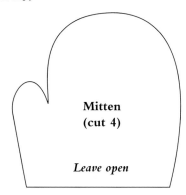

Mitten (cut 4)

Leave open

F O U R   Cut several long strands of yarn for the mustache and tack them below the nose.

F I V E   For eyebrows, cut two strands of yarn, each twice as long as the finished eyebrow will be. Fold the ends to meet in the middle. Hold the eyebrows gently in place with the cut ends underneath and overcast, passing the needle through the top strand instead of all the way over it.

Santa's Pack

O N E   Cut straight across the sock designated for the pack just below the heel (fig. g). Make a narrow hem around the cut edge. Sew the six small gold rings evenly spaced around the top of the bag, about ¾" (2 cm) from the edge.

T W O   For the drawstring, cut several strands of embroidery floss, each about 39" (1 m) long. Tie one end of the combined strands to something thin and stable (or have someone hold the end for you). Twist the strands in one direction until they begin to kink up when you release the tension. Hold the twisted length in the middle and double one half over the other, allowing them to twist together. Thread the drawstring through the rings, knot the ends together, and trim.

T H R E E   If you don't intend to fill the bag with real gifts or candy, you can fill most of it with stuffing and place several miniature toys and gift-wrapped squares on top.

Heidi the Downhill Skier

LET'S SEE…SKI SWEATER AND HAT, TIGHTS, SKI BOOTS, SKI POLES—YEP, SHE'S READY FOR THE SLOPES. THIS VARIATION ON FERGUS THE FISHERMAN TAKES FULL ADVANTAGE OF A COLORFULLY PATTERNED PAIR OF SOCKS.

SOCK TIP:

Be sure the socks for the sweater and hat have no printing on the feet and that the uppers of the socks for the body and sweater are at least as long as the feet.

SOCKS

1 sock for the body, size 9–11

1 pair of colorful "ski sweater" socks, size 9–11

1 sock for the head, size 5–6½

NOTIONS

Matching thread

Stuffing

1.5 oz. (42 grams) of yarn for hair

Hair loom (see page 15)

Hot-glue gun (optional)

8" (21 cm) square of felt for boots

Yarn for tassel

Embroidery floss or paint for face

For poles, 30" (77 cm) of ⅛" (0.5 cm) doweling, wheel macaroni, and model paint

Head, Body, and Boots

Follow the instructions for Fergus, but take the body of the sweater from the upper of one "ski sweater" sock and the arms from its foot. (The upper of the matching sock will make a colorful stocking cap.)

Hat

O N E Free the second upper from the rest of the sock. Turn it wrong side out. Without cutting the ribbing, trim the upper to form a stocking cap with the point of the cap near the cut edge. Round the point so that it will turn right side out easily after sewing (fig. a).

T W O Backstitch a seam around the cut area. Turn right side out and fold up a cuff. Make a small pom-pom or tassel from yarn or sew on a purchased one.

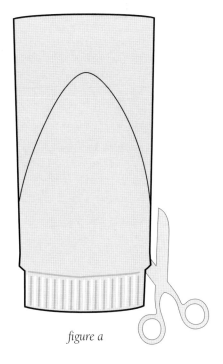

figure a

Stores that supply needlepoint materials are a good source for small amounts of yarn in a broad range of colors for the pom-pom or tassel.

Hair and Face

O N E Measure from an imaginary center part line to where you want the ends of the hair to fall. Double the measurement for the length of each strand of yarn. To determine the length to weave the wig, measure the length of the part from forehead to crown and double it. On the hair loom, make two weavings of this length (see pages 15–16).

T W O Remove the first weaving from the loom and tie the ends of the carpet thread together. Flatten this loop of yarn and lay it on the part line. Overcast it in place, catching the head and both sides of the loop (fig. b).

T H R E E Holding the first layer of hair out of the way, overcast the second loop just underneath it (fig. c). Using a backstitch or hot-glue gun, attach the under layer of hair to the head where a natural hairline would be (fig. d). Smooth both layers down and trim the ends (fig. e).

F O U R For bangs, make a short coil around a ruler as for making curly hair, attach it to the forehead, and then clip the ends to allow them to lie flat. Trim if necessary.

F I V E Paint or embroider the face.

Ski Poles

Cut two pieces of doweling each about the length of the doll and glue a piece of wheel macaroni 1" (2.5 cm) from one end of each. (I painted the poles in the photo with gray enamel model paint.)

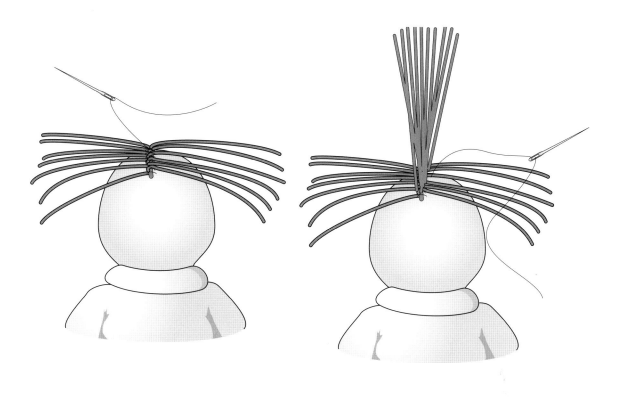

figure b

figure c

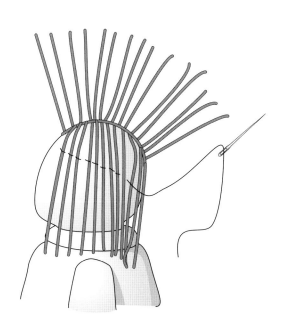

figure d

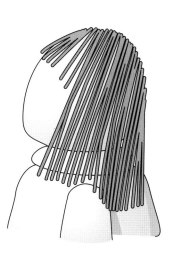

figure e

So Big the Bear

SMALL ARMS LOVE TO HUG THIS SQUISHY, PINT-SIZED BEAR, THE PERFECT COMPAN-ION FROM THE CRIB UP. ALTHOUGH YOU MIGHT ENJOY STITCHING HIM A WARDROBE, LIKE MOST BABIES HE LOOKS JUST AS GOOD BARE. WHEN YOU'RE SOCK SHOPPING, THINK ABOUT MAKING SO-BIG IN FANTASY BEAR COLORS AS WELL AS IN THE SHADES BEARS NATURALLY COME IN.

SOCKS

1 pair of soft, synthetic, smooth-knit children's knee socks

NOTIONS

Matching thread

Stuffing

Ribbon

Embroidery floss for face

figure b

Head, Body, and Rear Legs

ONE Stuff the toe of one sock to make the head (see fig. a). (If you make So Big a young bear, he can have a child-shaped head, as in the photo.) Prepare the head and neck according to the basic instructions (fig b). Set aside.

TWO Fold the other sock (see fig. c) so that the instep is facing up with the heel centered

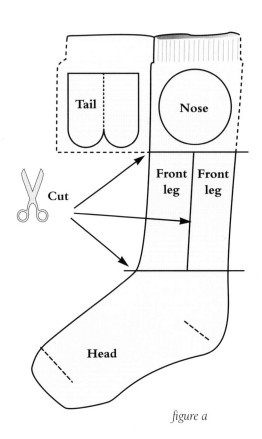

figure a

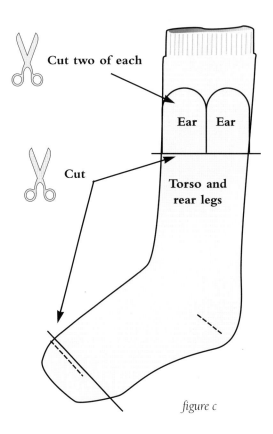

figure c

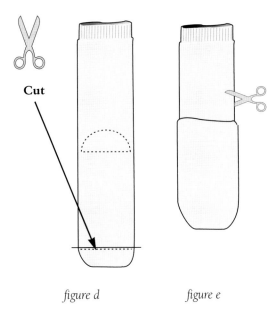

Cut

figure d　　　　*figure e*

FIVE Stuff one foot. Weave a straight pin across the foot just above the stuffing. (This will allow you to sew the feet into a forward position more easily.) Repeat for the other foot. Continue to stuff both legs. Weave a pin across the top of each. Stuff the body.

SIX Remove the pins in the feet. Bend one foot forward and ladder stitch it into position, going across twice for strength. Knot off. Repeat for the other foot. Remove the leg pins and sew a single line of running stitch across the top of each leg.

SEVEN Adjust the length of the body if necessary. Run a gathering stitch around the top of the body and seat the head. Pull the gathering stitch up, tucking in the seam allowance. Ladder stitch the head to the body and knot off.

underneath. Remove the toe with a straight cut just above the toe seam (fig. d). At the heel, fold the foot of the sock over the upper. Make a straight cut across the upper, ½" (1.5 cm) beyond the cut edge of the foot (fig. e). Unfold the sock, leaving the instep facing up. Reach under the sock and fold the heel toward the foot.

Front Legs

ONE Lay the ribbing and remainder of the body sock on top of the ribbing and remainder of the head sock (fig. h). Make a straight cut across the head sock where the raw edge of the body sock falls. Make another straight cut across the head sock just above the heel. Cut

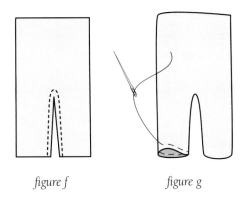

figure f　　　　*figure g*

THREE To make the rear legs, cut up the middle of the upper from the raw edge to within ½" (1.5 cm) of the heel. Turn wrong side out. Backstitch up one leg, across the crotch, and down the other leg (fig. f). Turn right side out.

FOUR For the feet, run a gathering stitch around the open end of one leg (fig. g). Pushing the seam allowance in, pull the gathering stitch up just enough to make a flat closure with rounded ends. Overcast across the opening and knot off. Repeat for the other leg.

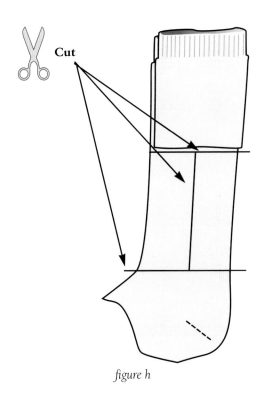

Cut

figure h

this tube made from the head sock up the center from raw edge to raw edge. (Each of the two resulting pieces will be one front leg.)

TWO Fold one leg right sides together and backstitch the long edge. Turn right side out. Run a gathering stitch around one open end. Push the seam allowance to the inside while gathering just enough to make a flat closure with rounded edges. (The long seam will run under the leg, and the flattened paw seam will run front to back.) Overcast the opening in this position (fig. i). Repeat for the other leg.

THREE Stuff each paw until it is firm. Weave a straight pin across each wrist (fig j). Continue stuffing the front legs until they are firm. Remove the wrist pins and turn the paws up. Ladder stitch each paw in place (fig. k).

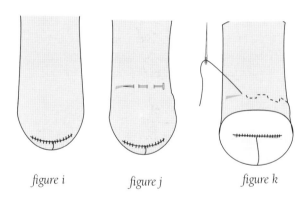

figure i   *figure j*   *figure k*

FOUR Adjust the length of the front legs if necessary. Run a gathering thread around the open end of one. Draw it up, turning the seam allowance in. Press the leg against the body at the shoulder so that the paw points up. Ladder stitch in a circle where the leg and body meet, going around twice for strength, then knot off. Repeat for the other front leg.

Ears, Snout, Tail, and Face

ONE Cut both pairs of ear pieces side by side from the fabric below the ribbing of the body sock (see fig. c). (If the socks are short, cut the ears, snout, and tail from the ribbing.) For the ears, cut out two pairs of elongated half circles.

TWO Place each pair of ear pieces right sides together and sew a narrow seam around the curve of each. Turn them right side out. Push the raw edges of the open sides in. Overcast these openings closed, then overcast the ears to So Big's head.

THREE Cut the snout and tail from the remainder of the head sock (see fig. a). For the snout, cut a circle whose diameter is a little more than half as wide as So Big's head. (You can trace around a small glass or a spice jar to get a perfect circle.)

FOUR Run a gathering stitch around the outer edge of the circle, leaving a narrow seam allowance (fig. l). Gently and evenly draw up the gathering until the piece forms a half-sphere. Stuff lightly. Overcast in place. Before sewing completely closed, stuff until firm (fig. m). Stitch closed and knot off.

FIVE Cut a short, rounded tail from the remaining piece of fabric (see fig. a). Fold with right sides together and sew the rounded edge. Turn right side out. Fold in the raw edge of the flat end and overcast the tail in place.

SIX Paint or embroider the face (here, I used satin stitch for the eyes and nose and added a light blush to the cheeks).

Finishing Touch

Tie a ribbon around the neck

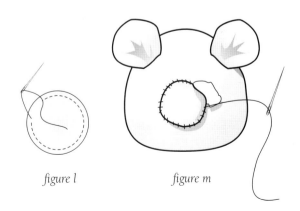

figure l   *figure m*

Ti Nee

A STURDY BABY DOLL IN OLD-FASHIONED
BOOTEES AND ROMPERS, TI NEE OFFERS
SWEET, SILENT, SOFT COMPANIONSHIP.
BECAUSE YOU CONSTRUCT A COMPLETE
BODY FOR THIS PROJECT BEFORE YOU SEW
ON THE CLOTHES, IT PROVIDES A TAKING-
OFF POINT FOR THE DOLL MAKER WHO
WANTS TO EXPERIMENT WITH REMOVABLE
CLOTHES. IF YOU PREFER SHOES TO
BOOTEES, CUTTING THE BOOTEES A LITTLE
LONGER AND LEAVING OFF THE RIBBONS
MAKES SOCKS PERFECT FOR PURCHASED
DOLL SHOES.

SOCK TIP:

The body socks and romper sock need to
have uppers as long as the feet.

SOCKS

1 pair of socks for the body, size 9–11

1 sock for the romper, size 10–13

NOTIONS

Matching thread

Stuffing

Yarn or embroidery floss for hair

Hair loom (see page 15)

Wide-toothed comb

Hot-glue gun (optional)

$1\frac{1}{4}$ yd. (1.2 m) of ribbon

Embroidery floss or paint for face

**Before you begin: Measure from the toe to
the heel on one of the body socks and note
this figure, which you'll use to measure the
arms later.**

figure a

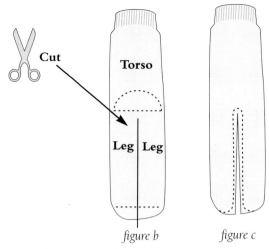

figure b   *figure c*

Head, Legs, and Body

ONE Stuff the toe of one of the body socks,
shaping a child-shaped head. Prepare the head
and neck according to the basic instructions
and set aside (fig. a).

TWO For the legs and body, lay the other body
sock so that the instep faces up and the heel is
centered out of sight (fig. b). Fold the heel
toward the upper. Cut up the middle of the foot
from the toe almost to the heel. Turn wrong
side out.

THREE Sew the leg seam, rounding the first
toe, moving up one leg and down the other,
and rounding the other toe (fig. c). Trim the
corners of the feet. Turn right side out. Stuff the
feet. Weave a pin across the top of each foot.
Continue to stuff the legs.

FOUR Bend one foot forward and slightly to
the outside of the leg, remove the pin, and sew
the foot in place using a ladder stitch. Repeat
with the other foot.

FIVE Bend one leg to the inside at the knee
area. Ladder stitch across the fold. (You may
want to leave one leg straight or sew both into
the bent position.) Stuff the torso with the legs
in a seated position.

SIX Check the proportion of the torso to the
legs and trim the torso if necessary. Run a gathering thread around the top. Seat the head and
pull the gathering up, pushing the seam
allowance to the inside. Ladder stitch the head
to the torso.

Arms and Hands

ONE For the arms, from the remaining upper
cut a length of tube based on the figure for the

arms you noted earlier (fig. d). Cut lengthwise up the middle of this piece through both thicknesses.

TWO Fold one arm piece wrong side out and sew the long side. Run a gathering stitch around the end where the hand is to be and draw it up. Turn the arm right side out. Stuff. Run a gather-ing stitch around the wrist and cinch it in. Repeat with the other arm.

THREE Adjust the arms for length. As with the legs, you may choose to sew one or both arms in a bent position. Set the arms aside.

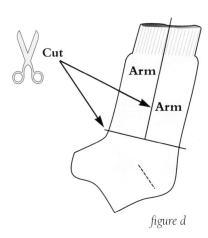

figure d

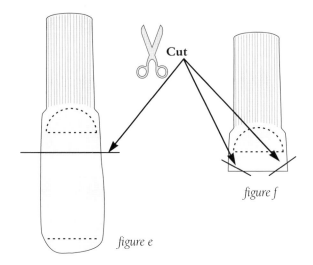

figure e

figure f

Rompers and Shoulders

ONE Fold the rompers sock so that the instep faces up and the heel is centered out of sight. Fold the heel toward the upper. Feel for the straight fold of the heel, measure down 2" (5 cm) from this, and make a straight cut across the foot (fig. e).

TWO Lay a ruler along the cut edge and mark ³/₄" (2 cm) in the center of the width of the sock. Mark up 1" (2.5 cm) on both outside folded edges. To form the crotch and leg holes, make one cut between the two points on the left and one between the two points on the right (fig. f). Turn the sock wrong side out and sew a ¼" (1 cm) seam across the crotch.

THREE Turn the sock right side out and pull the rompers onto the body. Turn the cut edges around the legs to the inside and adjust the position of the rompers, with the excess sock smoothed over the head. Hold two fingers of one hand inside the sock to prevent cutting the doll and trim the excess down to about ¼" (1 cm) above the neckline.

FOUR Run a gathering thread at the neck, catching only the rompers. Draw the gathering up, turning the raw edge to the inside, and ladder stitch the rompers to the head. Sew the leg edges to the body with an overcast stitch.

FIVE (optional) To make cuffs for the rompers legs: Measure 1" (2.5 cm) down from the finished edge of the leftover ribbing (fig. g). Cut straight across. Cut this piece in half to make two long rectangles. Fold each piece with right sides together and sew a seam on the 1" (2.5 cm) side of each. Push these bands of ribbing against the rompers legs, folding the cut edges under. Sew around both sides of each band.

SIX For the sleeves, measure down 2¼" (6 cm) from the cut edge of the leftover foot piece (fig. g). Make a straight cut across. Cut this piece in half lengthwise through both thicknesses. Fold each piece wrong side out and sew a seam on the 2¼" (6 cm) side of each. Turn right side out.

SEVEN Pull the sleeves onto the upper arms so that one cut edge of the sleeve is even with the cut edge of the upper arm. Turn the lower edges under ¼" (1 cm) and overcast them to the arms.

EIGHT Add enough stuffing to the arms to form shoulders when they are attached to the body. Run a gathering stitch around the open end of one arm and through both fabrics. Draw the gathering stitch up, tucking the seam allowance to the inside. Attach the arm by overcasting across the arm opening, catching the body and both sides of the arm opening. Overcast down one side of the arm for a short distance, ladder stitch under the arm, and overcast back up the other side to the top. Go around twice for a strong seam. Repeat with the other arm.

Hair

ONE Cut strands of yarn or floss about 7" (18 cm) long. (The doll in the photo has a wig of dark brown embroidery floss.) Weave two wig pieces on the hair loom, each about 4" (10 cm) long (see pages 15–16).

TWO Tie the ends of the carpet thread of one wig piece, flatten the circlet, and sew it to the part line. Use an overcast stitch and catch both sides of the weaving as well as the head (fig. h). Knot the ends of the carpet thread on the second

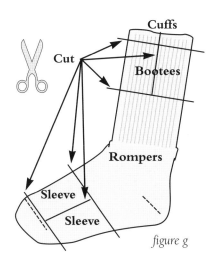

figure g

weaving and, holding the first layer up, overcast the second layer just beneath the first (fig. i). Comb all the hair down gently with a wide-toothed comb and trim the hair (fig. j). Lift small sections of hair, apply a thin line of hot glue to the head at the natural hairline, then replace each section. (Or sew the hair to the head at the natural hairline, using an overcast stitch.)

Bootees and Face

ONE Measure and cut a tube 2¾" (7 cm) long from the leftover upper (fig. g). Cut this piece in half through both thicknesses. Fold ¼" (1 cm) of fabric to the inside on one long side of each bootee (fig. k). (This fold should be on a side that runs perpendicular to the ribbing; it becomes the hem of the bootee.)

TWO With that fold in place, fold one piece in half with right sides together and pin. Starting at the hem, sew the side opposite the second fold, round the corner, and sew the adjacent side (fig. l). Repeat for the other bootee.

THREE Overcast loosely around the cut edge of each hem, catching the body of the bootee in each stitch (fig. m). Turn both bootees right side out. Tack the center of a 15" (38.5 cm) piece of ribbon to the seam of each bootee. Pull the bootees onto the baby so that the seam is at the back of the foot. Tie the ribbons at the front of each foot and trim any excess.

FOUR Paint or embroider the face.

Finishing Touch

Cut a length of ribbon trim for the rompers and tack it at the back and sides.

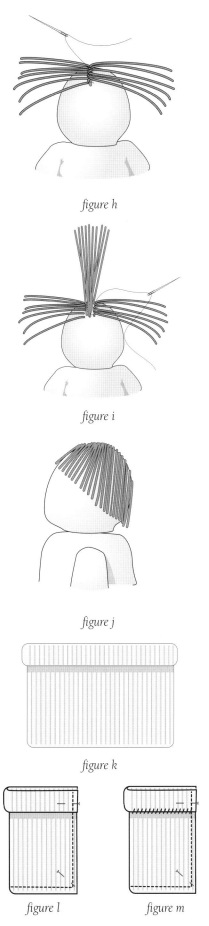

figure h

figure i

figure j

figure k

figure l   figure m

Pearl

A WELL-ROUNDED WOMAN, PEARL IS
DRESSED FOR SUCCESS—AS MOTHER,
CAREER WOMAN, CONFIDANT, OR ALL
THREE. SHE CAN ALSO AGE GRACEFULLY TO
BECOME A GRANDMOTHER OR A MRS.
SANTA. THIS PROJECT INTRODUCES A
TECHNIQUE FOR MAKING SLENDERIZED
LEGS AND ALLOWS FOR WARDROBE
CHANGES.

SOCK TIP:

The socks used for the ensemble and the
body should have uppers as long as the
feet. On the socks intended for the
ensemble, the pattern on the instep
doesn't need to extend under the foot.

SOCKS

1 smooth-knit sock for the body, size 9–11

1 pair of patterned socks for the ensemble, size
9–11

1 sock for the head, size 5–6½

NOTIONS

Matching thread

Stuffing

1.5 oz. (42 grams) of yarn for hair

Hair loom (see page 15)

Wide-toothed comb

Three beads for earrings and purse

Strand of small bead trim

6" (15 cm) square of thin black felt or leather
for shoes

Paint or embroidery floss for face

Head, Body, and Legs

O N E Stuff the toe of the sock intended for the
head, molding it into a slender egg shape.
Prepare the head and neck according to the
basic instructions (fig. a). Set aside.

T W O Fold the sock for the body so that the
instep faces up and the heel is out of sight (fig.
b). Remove the toe just above the toe seam.
Fold the heel toward the upper to prevent cutting it. To separate the legs, cut lengthwise up
the middle of the foot from the raw edge,
almost to the heel.

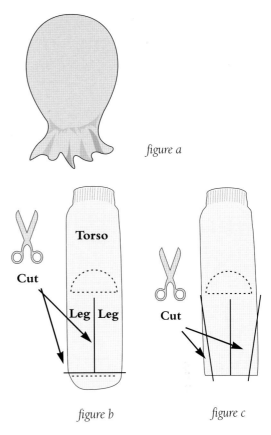

figure a

figure b   *figure c*

T H R E E At the bottom of each leg measure ½"
(1.5 cm) in from the fold at each outer edge
and make a pencil mark (fig. c). Place a ruler on
the sock so that it connects the pencil mark at
the bottom of the leg with the outside fold at
the hip area. Make a light pencil line. Repeat
this procedure with the other leg. Cut along
these lines. Trim to round the feet.

F O U R Turn wrong side out. Pin. Sew a narrow
seam that runs from one hip around the legs to
the other hip (fig. d). Turn right side out. Stuff
about 1¼" (3.5 cm) for each foot and weave a
straight pin across the top of each. After starting
to stuff one leg, hold the foot in a forward

figure d

87

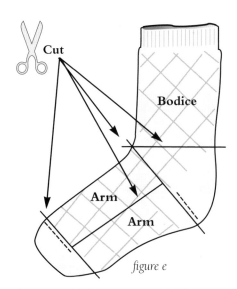

figure e

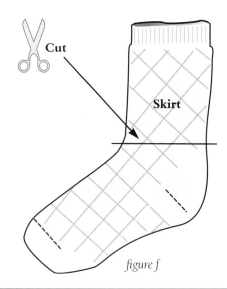

figure f

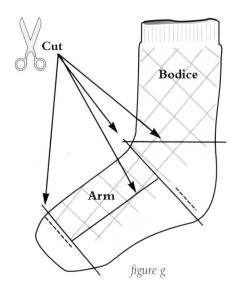

figure g

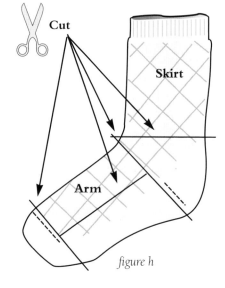

figure h

position. (When the feet are ladder stitched in place, they should extend 1" [2.5 cm] forward of the stitching.) Adjust if necessary. Finish stuffing the legs and torso.

FIVE Bend the feet forward and sew them in position with a ladder stitch. Before knotting each one off, take a couple of stitches back and forth through the ankle to slenderize it. Make dimples at the knees with a few back-and-forth stitches in the same manner.

SIX Trim the torso if necessary to make it more proportional to the legs. Run a gathering stitch at the top and seat the head. Pull the gathering up, tucking the seam allowance to the inside. Ladder stitch the head to the body. Run a gathering stitch around the waist and cinch it in.

Bodice and Skirt

ONE With straight cuts, remove the uppers from both decorative socks just above the heels (figs. e and f for socks with patterns all the way around the foot; figs. g and h for socks with patterns only on the top of the foot). One upper will be the bodice with the ribbing providing a rolled collar, and the other upper will be the skirt with the ribbing providing a waistband. Pull the bodice and skirt onto the doll and mark adjustments for the length of each. Allow for ½" (1.5 cm) hems. Remove both pieces and sew the hems with an overcast stitch. Take the needle deeply into the hem, but only pick up a tiny stitch on the outside fabric.

figure i

figure j

TWO Either sew the skirt to the body and the lower edge of the sweater over that or leave the lower bodice and skirt unattached to the body, so that later you can interchange skirts.

Hands and Arms

ONE For the hands, cut two rectangles from the remainder of the sock used for the head, each 2 x 1½" (5 x 4 cm). Stretch should be across the long side.

TWO With right sides together, fold each piece to form a 1 x 1½" (2.5 x 4 cm) rectangle. Sew a narrow seam up the side opposite the fold. Run a gathering stitch around one end, draw it up, and knot it off. Turn right side out and stuff. Repeat for the other hand (fig. i).

THREE If the pattern goes all the way around the foot on the decorative socks, one sock will provide enough fabric for the arms. Fold the sock so that the instep faces up. Remove the toe just above the toe seam. Refold the sock so that the heel is to one side and make a straight cut just below the heel to remove the foot tube (fig. e). Cut the tube in half lengthwise.

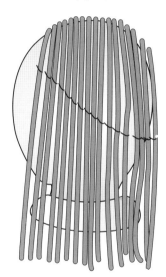

figure k

FOUR Alternative to step 3: If the pattern does not go all the way around the foot, free both foot tubes (step 3), then use only the instep from each sock (figs. g and h).

FIVE Fold each arm piece with right sides together. On one piece, backstitch a seam on the long side. Turn right side out. Run a gathering stitch around one end. Insert the unfinished end of one hand and draw the gathering up, pushing the seam allowance inside. Ladder stitch the hand to the arm and knot off. Repeat with the other arm. Stuff both arms.

SIX Adjust the length of the arms if necessary for more graceful proportions. Run a gathering stitch around the upper end of one arm and pull it up slightly, tucking the seam allowance

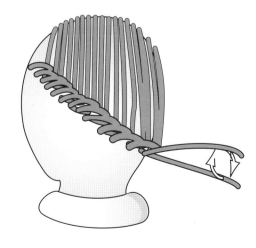

figure l

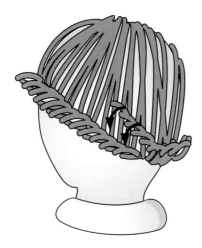

figure m

inside. Overcast the arm to the body, working across the top and down one side. Ladder stitch under the arm, overcast up the other side, and knot off. Repeat for the other arm.

Hair and Face

ONE Cut yarn into 10" (26 cm) strands and knot them onto the hair loom for a length of 4" (10 cm) (see pages 15–16). Remove the wig from the loom and tie the ends of the carpet thread together to form a circlet of knotted hair.

TWO Flatten the circlet into a straight line and overcast it to the head on the part line, catching the knots on each side and the head fabric (fig. j). Comb the yarn out with a wide-toothed comb. Starting close to the part, backstitch around the head to create a hairline (fig. k). Knot off.

THREE Roll the hair by twisting several strands up and around one another, starting at each side of the part and working toward the back (fig. l). At the back, trim the hair at an angle and tuck each end inside the opposite roll (fig. m). Pin. Overcast the hair tightly in place.

FOUR Paint or embroider the face.

Shoes and Purse

ONE Trace the two shoe patterns onto a piece of paper. Cut out the pattern pieces and pin them onto the thin felt or hold them against the leather while cutting. Cut two of each piece.

TWO With small overcast stitches, sew lines AB together on one shoe. Align both B points on the shoe upper with point B on the sole and overcast the sole to the shoe upper, matching

Patterns
(actual size)

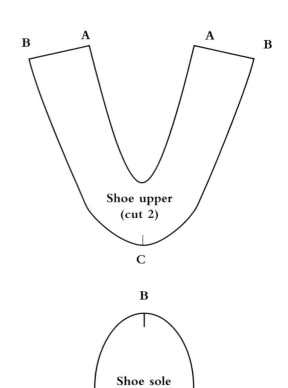

Shoe upper
(cut 2)

Shoe sole
(cut 2)

points C. Ease in the extra fabric of the shoe upper, especially while rounding the toe. Knot off. Repeat for the other shoe. Use a needle to lever the doll's heels and toes into the shoes. Tack the shoes to the feet.

THREE To make the purse, cut a 1½ x 2¼" (4 x 6 cm) rectangle from the fabric used for the shoes. Fold up a little more than one-third of the piece and overcast both side seams. Sew a bead onto the lower front of the envelope and make a thread loop on the upper flap that will go around the bead and hold the purse closed. Tuck a tiny handkerchief inside, if you wish.

Finishing Touches

Stitch beads into position for the earrings. Tack a strand of plastic bead trim at the neck.

The Auburn Family

REDHEADS UNITE! EACH MEMBER OF THE AUBURN FAMILY IS A VARIATION OF ONE OF THE OTHER DOLLS IN THE BOOK.

Mrs. Auburn

Mrs. Auburn is a variation of Pearl.

Mr. Auburn

Mr. Auburn is a variation on the Fergus the Fisherman design. He can be made in the same size socks as Mrs. Auburn and then stuffed for length, or, as in the photo, he can be made in socks one size larger. Omit the step in Fergus for tying off the legs and stuff them after attaching the boots. Make and stuff the boots and insert them in the trouser legs, turning up a small hem on each pant leg. Sew the pants around the outside of the boots. For shoelaces, use the instructions for the Patriotic Pals. Here I embroidered Mr. Auburn's hair, taking tiny stitches at the part and the hair ends to hold each strand.

The Auburn Teenager

The older sister calls for the Sweater Set directions and child-sized socks. For a doll about the size of the one in the photo, use size 5–6½ socks. Substitute 1½–2" (4–5 cm) rectangles to make the hands. Use the Sweater Set directions for the pony tail—you might try heavy crochet cotton for a straight, swingy look.

Auburn Baby

This infant was created from a pair of size 0–3 months baby socks with turned heels and a 0–3 months baby sock for the head. In the basic instructions for Poppy, substitute a 1¼ x 1¾" (3.5 x 4.5 cm) hand measurement and stuff to proportion. (I left the sock lace on the bonnet but removed it from the ruff.)

Costume Kids

Here's where imaginations can run wild. These dolls lend themselves to a world of scenarios—Halloween, plays and stories, untold numbers of adventures and dramas. Combine the instructions for the basic figure with a little ingenuity to create pastel rabbits for Easter, bears and birds, cats both domestic and wild, or fantasy and fairy tale creatures.

Sock Tip:

If you use a crew sock for the body, the arms can be on the ribbed area and the hands on smooth knit. If you use a smooth-knit sock with narrow ribbing, the arms will be smooth and the hands can be ribbed.

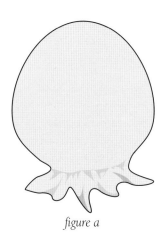

figure a

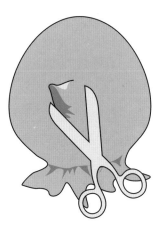

figure b

Lion Kid and Costume

Socks

1 pair of socks for the body, size 9–11

1 sock for the head, size 9–11

Notions

Matching thread

Stuffing

Yarn for mane and tail tip

5" (13 cm) square of felt or leftover socks for ears

Embroidery floss or paint for kid face

Dinosaur Kid and Costume

Socks

1 pair of socks for the body, size 7–8½

1 sock for the head, size 7–8½

Notions and Tools

Matching thread

Stuffing

2 pieces of felt, 12 x 9" (31 x 23 cm), or an equal amount of fabric for bill and tail

1 contrasting piece of felt for bony plates, 12 x 9" (31 x 23 cm)

1 piece of very stiff interfacing for the bill

Tiny bits of felt or paint for dinosaur eyes

Embroidery floss or paint for kid face and dinosaur nose

Hot-glue gun

Cardinal Kid and Costume

Socks

1 pair of red socks for the body, size 5–7

1 sock for the head, size 5–7

Notions

Matching thread

Stuffing

1 piece of red felt for wings, tail, and crest, 12 x 9" (31 x 23 cm)

Small pieces of black and gold felt for mask and beak

6" (15 cm) of cord elastic

Embroidery floss or paint for kid face

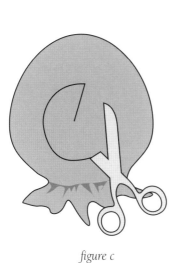

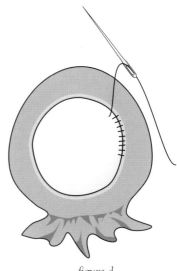

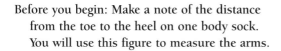

figure c

figure d

Before you begin: Make a note of the distance from the toe to the heel on one body sock. You will use this figure to measure the arms.

Head for All Kids

O N E   Stuff the toe of the head sock as for a child figure. Prepare the head and neck according to the basic instructions (fig. a). Push the head into the toe of one body sock. The front of the head should be covered by the seamless side of the toe. Run a gathering stitch around the body sock at the neck, draw it up, and knot off. Trim the body sock, leaving about ½" (1.5 cm) of fabric below the gathering.

T W O   In the center of the face pick up the body sock only, hold it away from the head, and make a small cut (fig. b). Then slide the scissors carefully under the colored sock and—leaving enough fabric to tuck under at least ⅛" (0.5 cm) all around—cut away a small circle to expose the face (fig. c). Overcast the opening to the face (fig. d). Set the head aside.

Legs and Body for All Kids

O N E   Fold the other body sock so that the instep faces up, with the heel centered underneath (fig. e). Fold the heel toward the upper. Starting at the toe, cut up the middle of the sock almost to the heel. Turn wrong side out.

T W O   Sew the leg seams, rounding one foot, moving up the leg, across the crotch, down the other leg, and rounding the other foot (fig. f). Turn right side out.

T H R E E   Stuff both feet. Weave straight pins

across the tops of the feet, then finish stuffing the legs. Sew the feet into a forward position with a ladder stitch.

F O U R   Stuff the torso, trimming the top of the sock to adjust for length if necessary. Run a gathering stitch around the opening. Seat the head. Draw the gathering up, tucking the seam allowance to the inside, and ladder stitch the head to the body.

Arms and Face for All Kids

O N E   Using the measurement you noted at the beginning of the project, cut a length of tube from the upper of the sock used for the hood. Cut up the center of the tube lengthwise

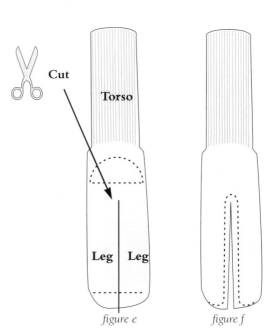

figure e

figure f

through both thicknesses, then fold each of these arm pieces with right sides together.

T W O   Stitch the long side of one arm. Run a gathering stitch around the hand end, pull the gathering up, and knot off. Repeat with the other arm. Turn both arms right side out and stuff. On each, run a gathering stitch around the wrist and cinch it in.

T H R E E   Check whether the arms are proportional to the body and trim them if necessary. Run a gathering stitch around the top of one arm and pull it up, pushing the seam allowance to the inside. Sew the arm to the body by overcasting across the top and down one side, then ladder stitching under the arm and up the other side. Go around a second time to make the seam more firm. Repeat with the other arm.

F O U R   Paint or embroider the face.

LION KID COSTUME

Ears

O N E   Trace and cut out the ear pattern. Cut four ear pieces from felt or leftover sock. (The ears on the costume in the photograph have fronts cut from a piece of smooth-knit sock and backs cut from a piece of ribbing.)

T W O   With right sides together, sew the ear seams. Turn right side out. Fold the open edges to the inside and overcast the ears to the head.

Lion Ear Pattern

(actual size)

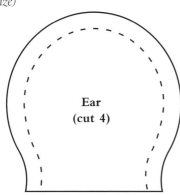

Ear
(cut 4)

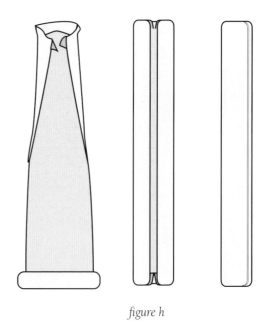

figure h

Tail and Mane

O N E Cut the tail as shown in fig. g, making it about 5" (13 cm) long and 1" (2.5 cm) wide. Prepare the tail as shown in fig. h: fold a narrow seam to the inside on each end, then fold the lengthwise seam allowances in, and then fold the tail in half lengthwise with the right side out and pin the long sides together.

T W O Overcast across one end and along the length almost to the tassel end. Lay in several loops of yarn for the tassel, then sew the end closed. Sew the tail to the body.

T H R E E For the mane, use the technique for curly hair described in the basic instructions. Sew two rows of loops around the head. The first row should be set back about ¼" (1 cm) from the edge of the hood and run forward of the ears. The second row should be just behind the first, behind the ears.

DINOSAUR KID COSTUME

Tail and Bill

O N E Trace and cut out the patterns for the tail and bill and pin them to felt or fabric. Cut two each. From the bill diagram trace a third pattern, making it ¼" (1 cm) smaller all the way around. (You can use the seam line to trace two of the sides.) From this pattern cut one piece of interfacing.

T W O With right sides together, sew around the tail. Trim the seam allowance. (If you are using felt, trim the seam allowance very close to the stitching.) Turn right side out. Use a strong needle to work the narrow end of the tail out. Stuff. Overcast the open end to the body, folding the seam allowance to the inside.

T H R E E To make the bill, center the interfacing on the wrong side of one bill piece and pin. Sew the pieces together, stitching ¼" (0.5 cm) in from the outside edge of the interfacing.

F O U R Place the bill pieces right sides together and sew around the outer curve ¼" (1 cm) from the edge. Trim the seam allowance and turn the bill right side out.

F I V E Turn in the seam allowance on the unsewn edge and pin the bill in place on the head with the interfacing stitching on the underside. Overcast the bill to the head.

S I X Make a pattern for the whites of the eyes by tracing the large eye circle and one for the

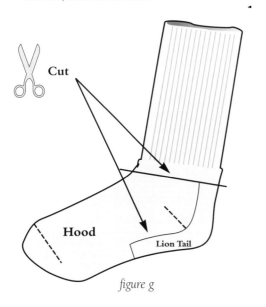

Cut

Hood

Lion Tail

figure g

Dinosaur Patterns
(50% actual size)

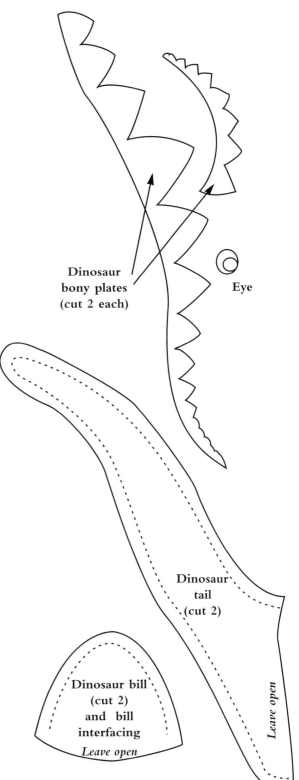

Dinosaur bony plates (cut 2 each)

Eye

Dinosaur tail (cut 2)

Leave open

Dinosaur bill (cut 2) and bill interfacing
Leave open

pupils by tracing the small circle. Use the large circle to cut two pieces from white felt. Cut two pupils from brown or black felt. If you are giving the doll to a young child, apply the eye pieces firmly by sewing on the whites first and then sewing the pupils onto them. For any doll owner not likely to eat the eyes, you can attach eyes with a hot-glue gun. With embroidery floss, make small stitches to represent nostrils.

Bony Plates

O N E Trace and cut out both pattern pieces for the bony plates and pin them to the contrasting felt. Cut two each. (It is easiest to cut each piece separately and then match them up.)

T W O Lay the two tail pieces together. Trim, if necessary, for a close match. Working only a small section at a time, run a thin line of hot glue along the zig-zag side. Don't glue the smooth side, or it will be hard to sew to the body. Trim away any leakage of glue after it has dried. Overcast the smooth edges to the doll's back and along the upper seam of the tail. Repeat this procedure with the head piece and sew the bony plates to the head.

CARDINAL KID COSTUME

Crest, Wings, and Tail

ONE Trace and cut out the patterns for the crest, wings, and tail and pin them to the red felt. Cut two crests, one tail, and one wing cape.

TWO Fold the arm casings on the wings over to the solid line on the pattern piece and sew them in place. Turn the wings over and pin the point of the tail in place on the wings at point A. At point B, pinch the sides of the tail in ⅛" (0.5 cm) on each side and pin. Sew the tail to the wings.

THREE Glue or sew the two crest pieces together and sew the crest to the top of the head.

Mask and Beak

ONE Trace and cut out the patterns for the mask and beak. (Depending on the face you've drawn or embroidered on your kid, the mask size and eyehole positions may need adjusting.) Cut one mask from black felt and one beak from gold felt.

TWO Sew one side of the beak to the nose arch of the mask. Fold the tabs on the mask to the back for reinforcement. Cut a piece of cord elastic to the needed length. Tie a knot at each end and take several stitches to tack the elastic to each side of the mask. Slip it over your cardinal kid's head.

Cardinal Patterns

(actual size)

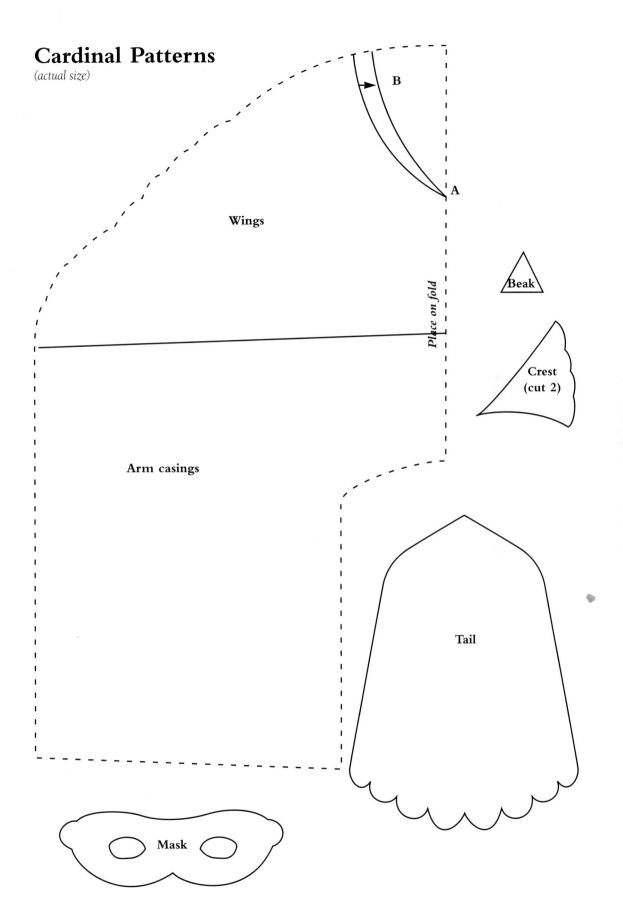

Wings

B

A

Place on fold

Beak

Crest
(cut 2)

Arm casings

Tail

Mask

Merry Anne

CLASSIC CHARM, CONTEMPORARY
APPEAL—A MEMBER OF THE FOLK-ART
FAMILY OF RAG DOLLS, MERRY ANNE HAS
AN IMPISH EXPRESSION, PETITE SIZE, AND
COLORFUL WARDROBE THAT GUARANTEE
HER POPULARITY. CREATING HER CALLS
FOR THE ECONOMIC USE OF TWO PAIRS OF
SOCKS.

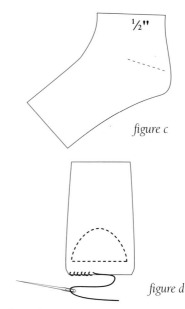

figure c

figure d

SOCK TIP:

Two pairs of anklets, two pairs of crew socks, or a combination of these socks will work for Merry Anne. Both pairs need uppers as long as the feet. The pair of socks used for the dress should not have synthetic elastic knitted in. For the doll pictured, I used a pair of heavy cotton anklets and a pair of finely knit crew socks. A good source of thinly striped stocking fabric is old knit shirts.

SOCKS

1 pair of white socks, size 6–7½
1 pair of colored socks, size 6–7½

NOTIONS

Matching thread

Stuffing

Striped knit fabric about the size of two sock feet laid side by side

1 yd. (.9 m) of ribbon for apron

18" (46 cm) of lace for apron (unless anklets have lace edging)

Ribbon for hair bow

1.5 oz. (42 grams) of yarn for hair

Embroidery floss or paint for face

Doll shoes

Before you begin: Cutting straight across, remove the ribbing from both white socks. Set the ribbing aside.

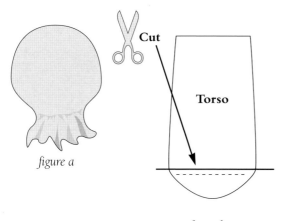

figure a

Cut

Torso

figure b

Head and Body

ONE Stuff the toe of one white sock. Mary Anne's head can be child-shaped or simply round. Prepare the head and neck according to the basic instructions. Set aside (fig. a).

TWO Fold the foot of the other white sock so that the instep is facing up, and cut off the toe just above the toe seam (fig. b). Refold the sock so that the heel is folded lengthwise. Cut straight across, trimming the upper to ½" (1.5 cm) above the heel area (fig. c).

THREE Fold the sock again so that the instep faces up and the heel is centered underneath. Tuck in the cut edge near the heel about ¼" (1 cm) all the way around. Overcast across the opening to complete the body (fig. d). (The heel will form the doll's bottom, and later you will sew the legs to the seam.) Stuff the body.

FOUR Run a gathering stitch around the top and seat the head. Pull the gathering up, tucking the raw edges inside. Ladder stitch the head to the body.

Legs and Feet

ONE Measure the length of the head and body combined. Then measure the width across the seam of the lower front of the body, double it, and add 1" (2.5 cm) for the seam allowances. Before you cut the striped fabric for the legs, be sure the stripes run along the width of the second measurement and that the stretch is in that direction also.

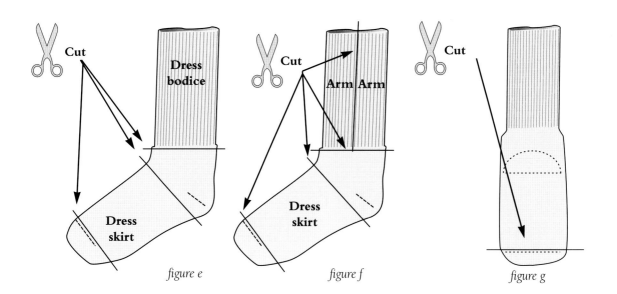

figure e

figure f

figure g

TWO From your two measurements, cut a rectangle of striped knit fabric for the legs. Fold the rectangle in half, with the fold perpendicular to the stripes. Cut along the fold.

THREE Fold one leg piece in half with right sides together, with the fold perpendicular to the stripes. Backstitch a ¼" (1 cm) seam along the raw edges, shaping a curve at one end for the foot. Turn right side out. Repeat for the other leg.

FOUR Stuff one foot firmly. Weave a pin across the top of the stuffed area. Stuff the calf and weave a pin across the top if it. Stuff the thigh, fold the raw edge in, and pin it closed. Repeat for the other foot and leg (see photo).

FIVE Removing the pins as you go, bend one foot forward and ladder stitch it in place. Sew across this seam twice, then knot off. Sew a running stitch across the knee bend and knot off. Overcast the opening at the top. Before you sew the leg to the body, be sure the leg seam is on the inside of the leg. Now overcast the top of the leg to the body seam and knot off. Repeat for the other leg, checking the seam position before you sew the foot in place.

Dress

ONE For the bodice, hold one colored sock upside down against the doll's body so that the finished edge of the opening falls just below the waist. Press the sock gently against the body, smoothing upward into the neck and up along the head. Mark this sock with a pin about ¼" (1 cm) above the neck.

TWO Remove the colored sock from the body and cut straight across the sock where the pin marks it (fig. e). (This straight tube is the bodice of the dress.) Run a gathering stitch around the cut edge. Pull the tube over the doll's head, finished edge first. Draw up the gathering thread at the neck, tucking in the cut edges, and ladder stitch the neck of the dress to the neck of the doll. Knot off.

THREE For the skirt, fold the foot of the other colored sock (fig. f) so that the instep faces up. Remove the toe by cutting straight across just above the toe seam (fig. g). Fold the sock to make a crease down the center of the instep. Cut straight across the sock just inside the lower heel area (fig. h). (Including a bit of the heel will make the skirt longer and provide some flare at the hem.) Repeat with the foot of the first colored sock (fig. e).

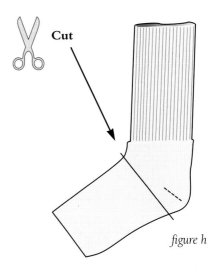

figure h

figure i

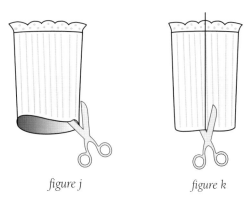

figure j   *figure k*

FOUR Cut lengthwise through a single thickness of each foot tube. Pin these two pieces with right sides together. (The cut edges from the heel form the hem.) Sew up each side. Fold under once or twice to create a narrow hem, then stitch.

FIVE Run a gathering stitch around the upper edge of the skirt, then pull the skirt onto the body and draw the gathering up, tucking the cut edge in. If the skirt looks short, stretch it gently or place it lower on the bodice. Be sure the seams are where you want them, then adjust the gathers at the waist so the skirt falls evenly and ladder stitch the skirt to the bodice.

Hands and Arms

ONE From white sock leftovers, cut two rectangles for the hands, each 1½ x 2" (4 x 5 cm)—the stretch should be along the longest side. Fold each piece right sides together to form a rectangle 1 x 1½" (2.5 x 4 cm).

TWO On one hand, backstitch a seam along the side opposite the fold to make a tube. Run a gathering stitch around one end of the tube and pull it up. Knot off. Turn right side out. Repeat for the other hand. Stuff both hands and set them aside (fig. i).

THREE For the arms, cut the upper from the other colored sock (fig. h). Cut this tube lengthwise up the center through both thicknesses. Fold one arm piece right sides together and backstitch the long side. Turn right side out. Run a gathering stitch around the finished open end. Insert the hand, draw up the gathering, and ladder stitch the hand to the arm. Knot off. Repeat for the other arm. Stuff both arms.

FOUR Adjust the length of the arms if necessary. Then turn in the raw edges at the top and overcast the arm to the body near the neck.

Apron

ONE Make the apron from the ribbed tops of the white anklets. If the ribbing has a lace edge, begin cutting where the ends of the lace meet and trim away the excess from either side. Cut lengthwise through one thickness of one ribbed tube (fig. j). Cut the second ribbed tube lengthwise up the center and through both thicknesses (fig. k).

TWO With right sides together, pin a smaller piece to each side of the larger piece of ribbing—make sure that all the finished edges run along the bottom of the apron. Backstitch both seams.

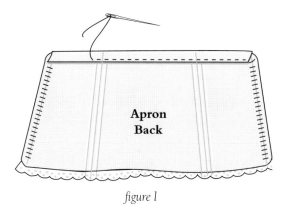

figure l

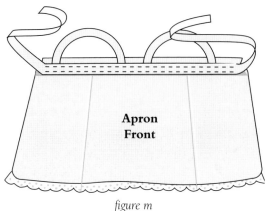

figure m

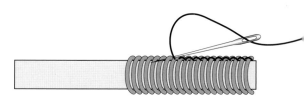

figure n

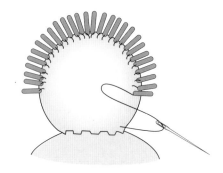

figure o

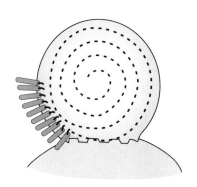

figure p

THREE Stretch the apron body gently and pin it to an ironing board, stretching the lower edges slightly wider than the upper edges. Iron it to eliminate the elasticity. Unpin.

FOUR Make narrow hems along the side edges. If lace didn't come on the socks, add a row of lace along the finished edge. Fold down a hem at the top and baste it in place (fig. l). (The sash will be stitched over the basting and the fold of the hem will show above the sash.)

FIVE For the sash, cut a length of ribbon long enough to go around the doll and to tie in a bow at the back. Pin the center of the sash in place at the center front of the apron. For the shoulder straps, cut two pieces of ribbon long enough to go over the shoulders. Tuck them into the sash at front and back, then pin them in place.

SIX Finish pinning the sash along the upper apron. If the apron is too big around, pull the basting up a little at the center. Machine stitch along the top of the sash. Trim the ends of the shoulder ribbons. Machine stitch along the bottom edge of the sash (fig. m).

Hair and Face

ONE Wrap yarn around a ruler for a length of about 6" (15 cm). With the yarn still on the ruler, backstitch along one edge (fig. n). Pull the yarn off the ruler and overcast it across the front of the head where you want the hairline to be (fig. o). Continue to work coils of the same length around the head, spiraling in and finishing at the crown (fig. p). Sew a bow to the head.

TWO Paint or embroider the face.

Finishing Touch

Add purchased shoes.

Margot the Ballerina

A SERIOUS BALLERINA IN HER PRACTICE
SKIRT AND TOE SHOES, MARGOT WILL
PIROUETTE HER WAY INTO THE HEART OF
A CHILD OR A COLLECTOR. HER GRACE-
FUL NECK, SHAPED LEGS, RIBBON SHOES,
AND DANCER'S HAIR MAKE MARGOT A
SOPHISTICATED PROJECT—ONE MORE EAS-
ILY CRAFTED AFTER SOME EXPERIENCE
WITH SIMPLER DOLLS.

Margot the Ballerina

SOCK TIP:

Three pairs of anklets and one pair of head socks will make two dolls. It's best to use cotton anklets without any synthetic elastic knitted in.

SOCKS

3 cotton ankle socks, size 9–11

1 sock for the head, size 5–6½

NOTIONS

Matching thread

Stuffing

1.5 oz (42 grams) of sport-weight yarn for hair

Hair loom (see page 15)

Wide-toothed comb

½ yd. (46 cm) of ribbon ½" (1.3 cm) wide for skirt waistband

1⅔ yd. (1.6 m) of ribbon ¼" (0.5 cm) wide for skirt ties and shoe ties

½ yd. (46 cm) of ribbon ⅞" (1.75 cm) wide for toe shoes

Embroidery floss or paint for face

Head

ONE Stuff the toe of the sock intended for the head, molding it into a slender egg shape. Make sure there is stuffing in the neck area before running the gathering threads. Start high at the back and, making small stitches, run a gathering stitch around the neck opening. Starting at the back of the head and about ½" (1.5 cm) below the first stitches, make a second line of neck gathering, then knot off (fig. a).

TWO Stuff the neck firmly. There should not be so much stuffing that it bulges or so little that it wrinkles. Trim the excess fabric. Stab stitch through the neck several times at the lower line of stitching to keep the stuffing in place. Set the head aside.

Legs and Body

ONE Fold all three anklets so that the insteps face up and the heels are out of sight. Remove the toe of each anklet by cutting straight across

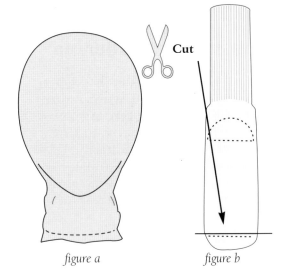

figure a

figure b

just above the toe seam (fig. b). Refold each sock so the heel is to one side again. Remove the foot tubes from two of the anklets by cutting straight across just below the heel (fig. c). (One of these tubes will become the legs, and the other, the arms.) Cut slightly farther into the heel of the sock that will provide the legs. On the third anklet, make a straight cut across the sock about ½" (1.5 cm) above the heel (fig. d). Set aside all three uppers.

TWO Cut up the center of the leg tube through both thicknesses (fig. c). Leaving the legs folded, measure in ½" (1.5 cm) on the lower end of the long cut side of each leg and make a pencil mark. Place a ruler on one leg so that it connects the pencil mark at the bottom of the leg with the top of the long, cut edge. Make a light pencil line along the ruler from top to bottom. Repeat this procedure with the other leg (fig. e).

THREE Cut along the ruled lines on both legs. Trim to round both feet. Turn the legs wrong side out and pin along the seams. Sew down the seam of one leg and around the toe. Repeat with the other leg (fig. f).

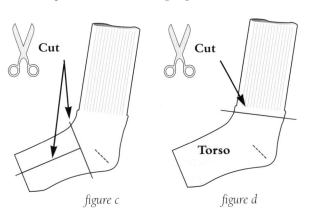

figure c

figure d

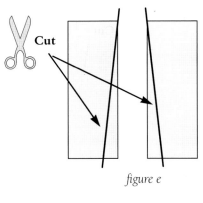

Cut

figure e

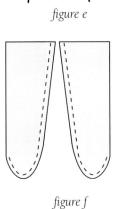

figure f

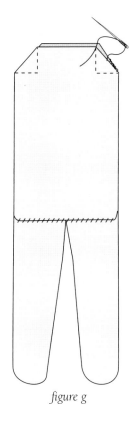

figure g

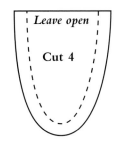

Hand Pattern
(actual size)

Leave open

Cut 4

FOUR Turn the legs right side out and stuff them. Turn the upper edges in and pin them closed. Set the legs aside.

FIVE Fold the anklet foot that includes the heel so that the instep faces up and the heel is out of sight. Fold in the cut edge nearest the heel about ¼" (1 cm) and, as you overcast this opening closed, work in a little gathering at each end. Draw the gathering up enough that the seam will accommodate the width of both leg tops. Knot off.

SIX Before you sew the tops of both legs to this seam, be sure the seam that runs down each leg faces to the inside. Now sew their tops to the overcast seam. (The heel forms the doll's rear.)

SEVEN Stuff the body. For this doll to be correctly proportioned, the legs should be longer than the body. Trim the body if necessary. To form the shoulders, fold in a dart on either side of the upper body (fig. g). Pin and sew the darts. Run a gathering stitch around the waist and cinch it in.

EIGHT Run a gathering stitch around the remaining opening. Be sure there is enough stuffing in the body to hold the head erect when the gathering is pulled up. Seat the head, turning the seam allowance in. Attach the head

to the body with a ladder stitch just above the lower row of neck gathering.

Hands and Arms

ONE Trace and cut out the hand pattern. Using the pattern, cut two pairs of hand pieces from the leftover head sock. With right sides together, sew each hand seam. Turn the hands right side out, stuff them, and set them aside.

TWO Using the same process as that for the legs, cut the last foot tube lengthwise up the center through both thicknesses for the arms. Leaving the arms folded, measure in ½" (1.5 cm) from one end of the long cut side of each arm and make a pencil mark. Place a ruler on one arm so that it connects the pencil mark with the other end of the long, cut edge. Draw a light pencil line along the ruler from top to bottom. Repeat this procedure for the other arm.

THREE Cut along the ruled lines on both arms. Reverse the folds on the arms so the right sides are together. Pin and backstitch the long, cut edge. Turn the arms right side out.

FOUR Run a gathering stitch around the narrow end of one arm. Turn the seam allowance in and tuck the open end of one hand into the arm. Pin it in place. Draw the gathering up and

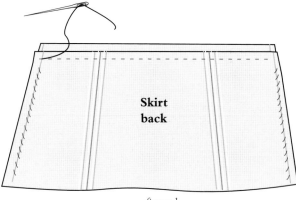

figure h

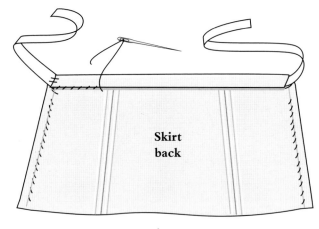

figure i

attach the hand to the arm with a ladder stitch. Repeat with the other arm and hand.

FIVE Stuff both arms firmly and set them aside. (Later, you can sew the arms to the body in any ballet position, but it works best to make the skirt and hair first.)

Skirt

ONE Cut lengthwise through one thickness of all three uppers. Hold one piece against the doll with the finished edge down and measure how long the skirt should be from waist to thigh. Using this figure, measure up from the finished edges of all three uppers and trim each piece to the correct length with a crosswise cut.

TWO Pin all three pieces in a line so that the finished edges form the lower hem and the two seams are on the inside of the skirt. Fold narrow side hems to the inside and pin. Sew both seams and both side hems.

THREE Stretch the skirt gently and pin it to an ironing board, with the finished edges stretched wider than the cut edges. Cover the skirt with a damp cloth and iron it. Let it cool before unpinning. (This process makes the ribbing less elastic.)

FOUR For the waistband, measure around the doll's waist one and a half times; add ½" (1.5 cm) to the measurement. Cut a piece of ribbon ½" (1.5 cm) wide to this length. Fold under each end of the ribbon about ¼" (1 cm) and iron.

FIVE Run a gathering stitch along the top of the skirt (fig. h). Lay the skirt along the ribbon, covering only half the ribbon's width. Draw the skirt up to match the length of the ribbon. Machine stitch the ribbon to the skirt. Fold the top half of the ribbon to the inside of the skirt and pin it in place.

SIX Cut two 14" (36 cm) lengths of ribbon ¼" (1 cm) wide for the ties. Tuck ½" (1.5 cm) of one into one end of the waistband and ½" (1.5 cm) of the other into the other end of the waistband. Pin.

SEVEN Sew one end of the waistband closed, stitching through the ribbon tie, and continue sewing along the inside of the waistband, attaching it to the inside of the skirt (fig. i). Finish by sewing the other end closed, stitching through the second ribbon tie. (You can wrap the skirt onto the doll with the overlap in the front or the back.)

Shoes

ONE For one shoe, cut 1½" (4 cm) of ribbon ⅞" (1.75 cm) wide. Cover the doll's toe with this piece running front to back, leaving more ribbon at the back than the front (fig. j). Tack the sides of the ribbon to the toe seam.

TWO Hold another piece of ribbon ⅞" (1.75 cm) wide and about 2" (5 cm) long around the foot and first ribbon, angling it high at the back and letting about ⅛" (0.5 cm) fall below the doll's toe (fig. k). Pin the ends of the ribbon together close to the foot.

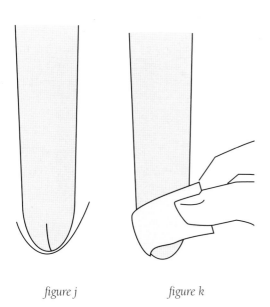

figure j · · · · · · · · · · · figure k

THREE Remove the ribbon from the foot and trim it to $\frac{1}{4}$" (1 cm) from the pin. With the ribbon folded so that the right sides are together, sew a $\frac{1}{4}$" (1 cm) seam. Trim the high point of the seam and overcast across the cutting line (figs. l and m). Turn right side out. Repeat these steps for the other shoe.

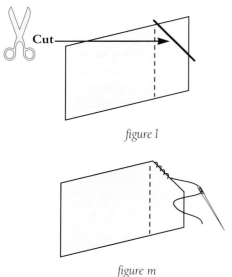

Cut

figure l

figure m

FOUR Cut a 14" (36 cm) length of ribbon $\frac{1}{4}$" (1 cm) wide for each toe shoe. Tack the midpoint of each ribbon to the top of each shoe seam on the outside. Pull the shoes onto the feet, leaving $\frac{1}{8}$" (0.5 cm) of ribbon below the

toe. With small stitches, overcast the upper edges of the shoes to the feet.

FIVE Run a small gathering stitch around the open end of one shoe. Gather this edge and then overcast it to the toe ribbon underneath so that a circle of toe ribbon shows, resembling the hard toe of a ballet shoe. Repeat for the other foot.

SIX Bring the tie ribbons to the front of each foot and cross them, then knot them at the back, trim, and tuck the ends in.

Hair

ONE Cut 14" (36 cm) strands of sport-weight yarn and knot these onto a hair loom to make a wig long enough to go around the head at the hairline (see pages 15–16). Remove the wig from the loom and knot the ends of the carpet thread to make a circlet. Pull the wig onto the head, pin it in place around the hairline, and overcast it to the head.

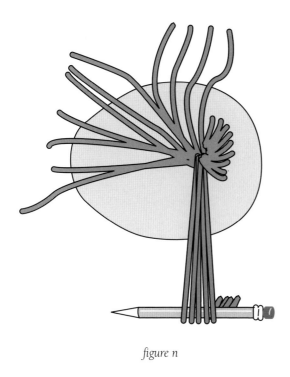

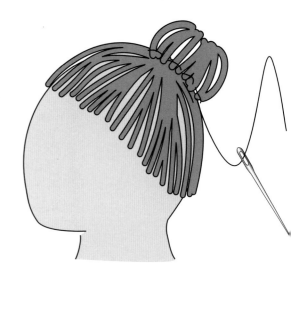

figure n

figure o

TWO With a wide-toothed comb, smooth the hair and gather it into a high ponytail. Run a gathering thread around the hair to pull it up, wrap the thread tightly several times around the gathering, and finish with several stab stitches through the ponytail. Knot off.

THREE Spread the hairs out evenly, letting them fall over the head. To make the bun, wrap small groups of hairs around a pencil, rolling them under tightly and tacking them at the crown (fig. n). Work around the ponytail in this fashion, keeping the hairs as smooth as possible. Trim the length if the coils are too bulky.

FOUR Finish by running a gathering stitch around the base of the bun and pulling it tight for a finished look (fig. o). Knot off.

FIVE Paint or embroider the face.

Finishing Touches

The arms can be attached in any ballet position. After deciding on placement, adjust their length. Run a gathering stitch around each arm opening. Before drawing the gathering up and tacking the seam allowance inside, make sure there is enough stuffing in the upper arm for Margot to maintain her pose. Sew around the arm-shoulder connection twice for firmness.

Epilogue

Imagination is the best toy we will ever possess, and the gifts of our hands are among the best gifts we can give. I delight in sharing the playful gift of these dolls with you and in knowing that you in turn may pass a portion of it on to someone else.

An original by Naomi F., age twelve

List of Suppliers

Ready-made doll shoes may be found at local doll or craft stores. The catalogues of the companies listed here include a variety of doll shoes and other accessories.

CR's Crafts
Box 8
109 Fifth Avenue West
Leland, IA 50453

Dollspart Supply Company, Inc.
46-50 Fifty-fourth Avenue
Maspeth, NY 11378

Pippin's Hollow Doll Supplies
23456 Mercantile Road
Beachwood, OH 44122

Standard Doll Company
23-83 Thirty-first Street
Long Island City, NY 11105

Tallina's Doll Supplies, Inc.
15790 S.E. Highway 224
Clackamas, OR 97015
(Include $1.00 for the color catalogue.)

Index